RURAL CRIME IN THE EIGHTEENTH CENTURY:
NORTH LINCOLNSHIRE 1740-80

B.J. DAVEY

THE
UNIVERSITY
OF HULL
PRESS

Cover Illustration:
The Denunciation by Hogarth
Reproduced by courtesy of the National Gallery of Ireland.

RURAL CRIME IN THE EIGHTEENTH CENTURY:
NORTH LINCOLNSHIRE 1740-80

B.J. DAVEY

THE UNIVERSITY OF HULL PRESS
1994

© **B.J. Davey**

British Library Cataloguing in Publication Data

A catalogue record for this book is available from the British
Library.

ISBN 0-85958-618-9
ISSN 0951-8916

Phototypeset in 11 on 12pt Plantin and printed by the Central
Print Unit, the University of Hull.

CONTENTS

Abbreviations

BL	British Library
LAO	Lincolnshire Archives Office
LNQ	*Lincolnshire Notes and Queries*
LRS	Lincoln Record Society
LRSM	*The Lincoln, Rutland and Stamford Mercury*

Lindsey quarter sessions records, in the Lincolnshire Archives Office, are referred to as follows:

Min.	Minutes of Lindsey quarter sessions
A55 etc.	LAO file reference number of quarter sessions rolls
Ep.	Epiphany
Ea.	Easter
M.	Midsummer
Mc.	Michaelmas

List of Maps and Tables

Acknowledgements

I should like to acknowledge the help I have received from the following friends and colleagues: Mr and Mrs T. Boundy, Dave Doyle, Jane Thomas, Roger Whyman. The Warden and fellows of Merton College, Oxford, gave me the opportunity of a study visit to complete some research. The staffs of the Lincolnshire Archives Office and Grimsby Public Library were helpful and efficient.

Mr Keith Scurr drew the maps and tables. I am especially grateful to Rex Russell and Jim Johnston, who both read early drafts and made valuable comments.

My greatest debt is to Dr Rod Ambler who suggested the book and did much editorial work to help me complete it. I thank all these people, but exempt them from any responsibility for the errors, which are entirely my own.

INTRODUCTION

Lindsey in the Eighteenth Century

This study is based on the records of the courts of quarter sessions for Lindsey between 1740 and 1780. Lindsey was that region of Lincolnshire beyond the Trent and the Witham, its coastline bulging into the North Sea from the Humber to the Wash. It was a large area, some fifty miles long and forty miles wide, yet in many places sparsely peopled: in 1801 there were 204,000 inhabitants spread over nearly a million acres of land. The sense of the place and its spaciousness are perhaps best caught by the old saying that it is 'two-thirds sky'.

In the eighteenth century there was still much wild country here. There were great, undrained Fens in the Witham valley, the Ancholme valley, and in the Isle of Axholme. The people in these places were reckoned to be 'mighty rude': fiercely independent fenmen living their own peculiar way of life; immigrants to the large fen-edge villages, attracted by the huge commons; and, especially in Axholme, hundreds of small freeholders. Many upland areas were still bleak and unproductive moor, given up to gorse and rabbits. The northern Wolds were 'a barren, thinly-peopled tract, much of it uncultivated'.[1] The prehistoric track which ran north-south along the Wolds, the Bluestone Heath road, was still lined with ancient burial mounds adding to the sense of wildness. In the north-west, around what is now Scunthorpe, there were great sandy heaths, where the dust storms reminded one visitor of

Arabia.[2] There was also much good farming country. All along the eastern coast was the Marsh, fifty miles long, five to ten miles wide, and some of the richest pasture land in England. Here grazed thousands upon thousands of sheep, and 'innumerable droves of red or red-and-white cattle'.[3] Much grazing land had been enclosed, piecemeal, since the middle ages. Elsewhere, villages were still cultivating the strips of their two or three open fields. In general terms Lindsey was a country of small farmers. On the Banks estate at Revesby in 1799 there were 268 tenants paying on average £22 p.a. rent; at Owersby well over half the Monson tenants held less than thirty acres of land.[4] There was wide variation, but most of these farmers grew wheat, barley, oats, and peas, and kept cows, horses, pigs, and sheep. Historians have echoed contemporaries in being impressed by their hard-headed, frugal way of life: their inventories show they held three-quarters of their wealth in farming stock and only ten per cent in household goods.[5]

The gentry avoided the Marsh and the Fens, preferring to congregate in the more healthy and attractive uplands. Ermine Street strikes north from Lincoln along a limestone ridge commanding mighty views over the Trent valley and giving easy access to the county town. Just off it, to the east, were to be found the classical mansions of some of the Whig gentry who ruled the county in the eighteenth century: the Monsons at Burton; the Wrays at Fillingham; the Saundersons at Glentworth; and the Whichcots at Harpswell. The Tories lived deeper in the countryside, in 'Spilsbyshire' at the southern edge of the Wolds. This was an area of chalk hills cut with small, winding, hidden valleys; a countryside of old lanes, covert woods and thick hedges. Here were the ancient manor houses of families whose Lincolnshire pedigrees stretched back over centuries: the Langtons, the Massingberds, the Dymokes.

Land here was cheap and beginning to attract wealthy merchants who wanted to set up as country gentlemen, like the Banks at Revesby. Families like the Pelhams at Brocklesby could accumulate vast estates. In spite of this, Lindsey was being deserted by its landed classes; it was too rural, too wild, too far from London. The dukes of Ancaster abandoned their old home in 'Spilsbyshire' to live south of Lincoln; the earl of

MAP 1
Lindsey

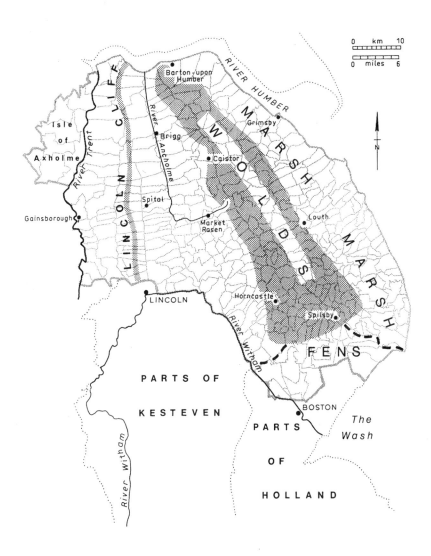

Scarborough gave up attempts to make Glentworth the capital of his estates. Thus Lindsey became a region of poorer gentry whose estates often 'did not extend much beyond their park gates'. Of the seventy landed gentlemen who lived in the southern half of the area, fifty had estates worth less than £200 p.a. and twenty-nine less than £100. About half of these were 'real absentees', and only nineteen of the seventy were permanently resident. Only twenty-nine of ninety-seven parishes had resident priests.[6] This meant that Lindsey was notoriously given up to the management of land agents and attorneys; and it was very difficult to find gentlemen willing to act as justices of the peace.

Towns were few, and small. The largest was Lincoln with about 4,500 inhabitants in 1750. Visitors were impressed by its site and its cathedral, but Gothic architecture was not fashionable in the early years of the century so the proliferation of churches and medieval stone buildings only added to a sense of battered decay. Gainsborough was a thriving river port trading down the Trent and Humber to the north sea. With about 3,000 people, it had outgrown its system of government and provided much work for the Lindsey justices. Louth, the capital of the Wolds, did not: although it had only 2,500 residents Louth was a borough, with its own quarter sessions. Beyond these three the market towns were tiny, even by the census of 1801: in the south, Horncastle's population had reached 2,000, but its neighbours, Alford and Spilsby, were only half that size. Farther north Market Rasen and Caistor had about 800 inhabitants. On the Humber, the little port of Barton grew to 1,500 in the eighteenth century, just outstripping the declining borough of Grimsby. As a borough, Grimsby could still exist from 'venality and corruption', but it also had its own quarter sessions, so, like Louth, it is omitted from this study.

For people of the eighteenth century, Lindsey was wild and remote. It was almost an island, guarded by the sea, the Trent, and the Fens. Even Lincoln was primitive: at the start of the century it had no theatre, no place of public assembly, no library (except the cathedral library), no coffee house, no printer; meetings had to be held in inns, and announcements were made by the crier with his bell. There was no regular stage-coach, and

London was three days' journey on horseback. Three times a week a postboy set out for Newark, to collect letters dropped by the northern mail.[7] Within the region, to travel was to battle with water, mud, and roads which were 'improved' by ploughing. One wealthy lady never ventured out unless her coach was pulled by four horses and equipped with cases of wine and sandwiches.[8] Tennyson's grandmother suffered agonies of travel sickness when she had to make the journey of eight miles to visit her mother; in winter she did not attempt it at all.[9] Many of the gentlemen unfortunate enough to have to spend the winter months in residence retired to their houses in the little towns where they remained 'shut up' until the spring.

This remoteness is one reason to study crime in the area. The recent interest in the history of crime has produced several major studies of counties in the south of England. There the system of criminal justice and the 'crime rate' could not avoid being influenced by the close proximity of London. Lindsey, three days' journey from the capital, and entirely rural, provides a contrast.

The Courts and their Records

We are fortunate in Lincolnshire that the Lincoln Record Society has published the *Minutes of Proceedings in Quarter Sessions* for the Parts of Kesteven in the late seventeenth century.[10] The editor's introduction, by S.A. Peyton, is an excellent reference work giving thorough details of the courts, their officers and procedures. Here, all that is attempted is a brief outline sketch as a first introduction to the system; as such it tries to select the main themes, and ignores many variations and possible alternative courses of action. The essential feature of the eighteenth-century system of law enforcement was that it was driven by private prosecution. If, as frequently happened, someone stole your washing from the hedge where it had been put to dry, it was up to you to find and apprehend the culprit. You might do this alone, accompanied by neighbours, or even with the assistance of the parish constable. The constable acted part-time, unpaid; he would have to leave his workshop or his fields and, unlike the modern police, he would not prosecute for you.

Having caught your criminal, the next stage was to take him before a justice of the peace. You, your witnesses, the accused and his witnesses, and perhaps the constable, trooped off to the house of the local justice. The justice had several alternatives. In minor matters, there might be a summary trial: the case was heard and determined immediately by the single justice acting alone. Usually, and probably in a case of stolen washing, the magistrate was not competent to try the case alone and he would refer the matter to a higher court. If the accused lived in the village and the case was not very serious, he would simply be bound over to appear: that is, he would have to find two respectable neighbours willing to stand sureties, usually of £20, forfeited if he did not appear. If the case was more serious, or it was feared the accused might abscond, he was committed to one of the houses of correction, at Louth or Gainsborough, to await trial.

Four times every year, at Epiphany (January), Easter (April), Midsummer (July), and Michaelmas (October), the magistrates met together in the court of quarter sessions to try these more serious cases, typically assaults and minor thefts. Many of the accused would be dismissed after answering to their bonds, or because the prosecutor had second thoughts, or because the two parties had reached agreement. Others, a minority, went for trial by jury. A significant difference in the eighteenth-century system was that first the evidence had to be outlined to a grand jury to be sure that there really was a case to answer. If so, the accused stood trial before a petty jury who delivered a verdict. If found guilty most convicts suffered a fine or flogging. Sessions was not only concerned with criminal business; after adjourning for dinner the magistrates remained at the inn to deal with administrative matters, mainly confirming the appointments and passing the accounts of parish officers, like the constables and overseers of the poor.

The most serious cases such as murder, robbery, theft of anything worth more than one shilling, were sent to assizes. Twice every year, in Lent (March), and Midsummer (July), the king's judges came to Lincoln to deliver those accused of such crimes from gaol. The proceedings were designed to impress: the judges were escorted to Lincoln, and the court opened, with great ceremony; most of the gentry attended to act as grand jurors, to transact important county business, and to grace the social functions which accompanied assizes. At the end, the rituals of the black cap or the white gloves signified whether or not there were to be public executions at the castle.

Lindsey had certain idiosyncrasies. The county of Lincolnshire was divided into three 'Parts': Holland, Kesteven, and Lindsey. Each of these Parts had its own quarter sessions. In most English counties quarter sessions were held in the county town, but the terrain and size of Lindsey made this impossible. Here in the early eighteenth century each sessions was adjourned to several different places, the clerk of the peace and other officers of the court carrying the king's commission to such towns as Horncastle, Gainsborough, Caistor, Louth, Spilsby, Alford and Spital each quarter.

Most of the records of Lincoln assizes in the eighteenth century have been lost. However, there is a good set of printed calendars for the 1770s, and although assizes dealt with the most serious cases these made up less than one-fifth of all crime. Most business went to quarter sessions and this study concentrates on the records of those courts between 1740 and 1780. They are of two types: the minutes, (the clerk's brief formal notes of proceedings and decisions), and the rolls. The rolls are the most fascinating and useful. At the end of each sessions the clerk rolled up all the documents produced by the court. Today each one of these rolls presents a glorious jumble of relics of the eighteenth century: bonds of thieves or men who beat their wives, statements by witnesses, formal indictments, life stories of vagrants, allegations of paternity, certificates, letters, excuses for avoiding jury service, details of punishments. Most of the rolls are in good condition: a few in the middle of the period have decayed, but most of the damage is to the more ephemeral paper documents; the formal, legal records were written on parchment, and they have survived.

These records are used to describe and examine changing patterns of crime in this remote rural area. But they can also tell us much more. First, the statements made by prosecutors, witnesses, and accused often give us much information about social life; indeed they are some of our only records of how the poorest people lived. Secondly, they are a record of government, in its widest sense: of how the community controlled its members, of the role played by parish officers, of the relationship between rulers and ruled. There is much to be learned about the attitudes of the magistrates who dominated the system. A central theme of this study is the transformation of rural government which took place in the middle years of the eighteenth century.

PART I. RURAL CRIME IN THE
EIGHTEENTH CENTURY

1 THE PROBLEMS OF THE 1740s

a) Instability

G.M.Trevelyan began his description of the middle years of the eighteenth century thus:

> The gods mercifully gave mankind this little moment of peace between the religious fanaticisms of the past and the fanaticisms of class and race that were speedily to arise and dominate the time to come.... (It was) a society self-poised, self-judged, and self-approved, freed from the disturbing passions of the past, and not yet troubled with the anxieties about a very different future which was soon to be brought upon the scene by the Industrial and French Revolutions.[1]

Trevelyan might have been able to use the work of modern historians of crime to support this familiar picture of the age. Most studies show a steady fall in the 'crime rate', or at least in the rate of prosecutions, in the first half of the eighteenth century.[2] The figures for Lindsey agree with this trend, and show a particularly sharp fall in the later 1740s. In seeking to explain this it is important not to use a circular argument to minimise the achievement, to say that it was easier for them to deal with crime because life was simpler then and times were more peaceful. Few contemporaries would have recognised Trevelyan's age of stability. The Lindsey gentleman of 1740, while he might have acknowledged that things had improved since his father's day, was still much troubled by the anxieties of the past. The past which tormented him was the seventeenth century, remembered as an age of civil war when tyrannical kings and puritan zealots had torn the country apart, and men had languished in ignorance, superstition, and the barbarism of unchecked 'enthusiasm'.

Progress had been made: the 'Glorious Revolution' of 1688 had guaranteed religious toleration, parliamentary government, and the safety of property. These gains had been confirmed by the acceptance of the Hanoverian kings in 1714, and the prolonged dominance of Walpole, 'no saint, no spartan, no reformer'. Some might even claim a new age of reason and toleration.

Yet the past was very real, and enough of it survived in Lindsey to bear witness to the terrors that had been and to present uncomfortable reminders of what lurked just below the surface of the new order. Most visitors to the county came through Lincoln which was one such reminder. The city had changed hands several times during the civil war, and the damage to churches and buildings was still evident in the early eighteenth century. In 1724 Defoe described it as 'an antient, ragged, decay'd, and still decaying city'.[3] Elsewhere the desecrated monuments and gaping blank windows of churches like Tattershall fed memories of the old struggles. Beyond the physical remains families like the Stovins or the Boucheretts were scarred by memories of persecution and suffering in the fanatical tumult of the seventeenth century.

Politics could still totter on the edge of violence. In 1722 the young Tory lord of Gainsborough, Sir Nevile Hickman, was so outspoken in his views on the government of the day that a rival told him 'his town deserved a troop of horse'. Hickman replied that if the gentleman was prepared to lead them 'he would head his'.[4] Hickman stood as the Tory candidate in the great county election in 1724 when the government determined to break the Tories in Lincolnshire and bring in a loyal candidate. The lord lieutenant, the duke of Ancaster, mobilised the Whig gentry, and in Lindsey the Whichcots, the Boucheretts, and the Pelhams vigorously canvassed the freeholders. When they went to Gainsborough they were mobbed in the streets 'and dirt thrown at them in a shameful manner'.[5] The result was close, but Hickman lost by 2,584 votes to 2,406 and the Whigs saw the vote as decisive, believing 'now it is not in the Power of the Torys ever to Chuse another Member for our County'. The Gainsborough people 'for their former insolence' were to 'have some Soldiers Quartered amongst them'.[6]

Many thought the victory of 1724 was more apparent than real and for many years Lindsey was popularly believed to be a hotbed of Toryism, or even worse. In the cathedral city of Lincoln, in the ancient manor houses of the southern Wolds there were clerics and gentlemen who were still uncomfortable with the new regime because it rested on the expulsion of an anointed king in 1688. In public they were Tory; in private, or in their cups after dinner, they still roared toasts to 'the king across the water', the exiled Stuart claimant to the throne. In reality that past was dead, but its ghost still walked, and in 1745 it came back to haunt them.

In the autumn of that year Charles Edward Stuart led his army of 5,000 barbarian Scots into England. By November they had taken Manchester and then, abandoning their artillery, they began a bewildering series of marches and counter-marches in the midlands. These tactics presented the Lindsey Tories with a stark choice: did they mean their words or not? With their Prince in Derby it was impossible to evade the issue.

The Whig Establishment was greatly alarmed. The lord lieutenant called a meeting of all the gentry and clergy of the county of Lincoln. They entered into an 'Association for the Security of His Majesty's Person and Government'. Over 200 people contributed to a fund for the defence of the county with the great aristocrats offering £500 each, the gentry £100 or £150, and many others contributing £5 or £10. The money was used to raise a regiment of volunteers who assembled at Stamford and marched north to assist in the defence of Hull. In every parish constables listed and required oaths of loyalty from, 'papists or reputed papists or persons disaffected to His Majesty's government'. Especially along the coast some of the magistrates led horse patrols to search the houses and outbuildings of such people. In Gainsborough all those who owned arms were called to meet in their churchyards with gunpowder and shot to resist the rebels if they tried to cross the Trent.[7]

By the first week of December the whole county was 'terribly alarmed'. Lord Monson found Lincoln in a state of panic. He wrote to his brother:

> 2 December. I ... went myself to Lincoln, where I found the whole city in the utmost confusion.
> 7 December. We have been all this week under continual alarms from the rebels. ... On Wednesday we had certain advice that they had got to Derby... The people of Nottingham flocked to Lincoln, and assured us they were marching this way, and would be here that night or next morning.[8]

But the rebels never did come to Lincoln. On 'Black Friday', 6 December, the Prince had ordered the retreat and by the spring his Scots had been slaughtered on Culloden Moor. The only real signs of battle in Lincoln were the wretched strings of prisoners who passed through the town, tied in couples and guarded by dragoons. By contrast, when 'Butcher' Cumberland sped through Stamford a mightily relieved gentry sent him a coach and six and he was ushered in 'with the ringing of the bells and the joyful acclamation of the people'.[9]

Above all, the '45 proved that the suspected or even self-proclaimed Jacobites in Lindsey were nothing more than loyal Tories, for they had not responded to their Prince's call. It is true that some families, the Hickmans, the Dymokes, the Massingberds, are strikingly absent from the list of subscribers to the lord lieutenant's fighting fund.[10] It is said that one of the Massingberds went to meet Charles Edward at Derby. But that was all. Otherwise the Tories did not stir and it is not difficult to find reasons. In April 1746 bonfires were lit all over the county to celebrate the victory of Culloden. At one of them, in South Kelsey, a labourer was arrested for suggesting that the company would be better setting fire to the barns of a local farmer.[11] That was the point. The Tory gentlemen had too much to lose. Who knew what terrors might be unleashed by prolonged civil strife? In this sense the Tory gentry valued the stability of the established regime as much as the Whigs, and the rebellion forced them to confess it. Many now positively supported it; by 1748 Hickman was an active magistrate.

The point to be made is that this happy conclusion, which was an important feature of the stability eulogised by Trevelyan, was far from certain in the early 1740s. Many magistrates, officers, and people of that age were anxious at the threats of faction, disorder, or even civil war.

b) Hardship

Economic prospects in Lindsey were similar to those for political stability. In the long term, the outlook was good: the growth of the textile towns in Yorkshire and improvements in transport promised rich markets for Lincolnshire wool and meat; the Fens and poor soils of the Wolds offered great opportunities for development by drainage and better farming practices. Already in the early eighteenth century progressive landowners like the Massingberds were showing what might be done, and the cheapness of land in Lindsey encouraged investment by successful tradesmen ambitious to become landed gentry.

As in politics, this future was not so readily apparent to contemporaries. For the poorest people conditions should have been better in the first half of the century: generally, prices were low while wages remained constant, at about eightpence or ninepence a day for labourers. However, this was a society which had no modern technology to protect it from full exposure to the elements and life remained a brutal struggle for existence in harsh and uncertain circumstances. The staple food was barley bread, and everyone watched the seasons anxiously, for bad weather might mean danger of starvation. The terrible winter of 1739-40 was a period of intense suffering, long recalled in popular memory as 'the great frost', when 'the fruits of the earth were destroyed by the cold ... and many persons were chilled to death. Trees split asunder .... Wells were covered with impenetrable ice ... and the poor were grievously afflicted'.[12] Distress bred crime as men stole to feed their families. The winter sessions for Lindsey that year condemned five men to transportation for stealing sheep, while the grand jury threw out charges against five more. Sheep theft did not reach such levels again for nearly a century and the fact that the cases were heard at sessions reflects the desperation of the thieves and the recognition by the magistrates that times were exceptional. Normally these men would have been sent to assizes and might have been condemned to death.[13]

Houses were of mud and stud, thatched. Where they were close together they burned uncontrollably with a regularity that is difficult to imagine today. Caistor, Louth, Market Rasen, Epworth, Binbrook and Barton all suffered major fires in this period. Poor housing was one factor in high levels of disease. Anxiety about the weather or failed harvests was perhaps exceeded by fears of epidemics, as uncontrollable as the fires. In 1728 a marshland clergyman wrote alarmingly of 'a very mortal distemper which carries off whole families in three or four days illness; their throats being generally sorr and their heads swelled to an uncommon size'. He had buried seven people in two small villages during the last week and was just going to bury a man whose wife he had buried a few days earlier.[14] Even in normal times in the first half of the century the death rate was 50 per 1,000 in the Marsh, and 35 per 1,000 on the Wolds. Approximately a third of all children died before the age of five, and almost a third of marriages were broken by premature death within fifteen years.[15] If there were benefits in falling prices and static wages they did not produce an increase in population. In Lincoln burials exceeded baptisms from 1711 to 1730 and only just matched them between 1730 and 1750. It is estimated that the population of Lincolnshire fell from 179,000 in 1700 to 153,000 in 1750. [16]

Of the small farmers, who were such a large section of the population of Lindsey, Arthur Young said they lived hard and fared hard. They were not wealthy enough to avoid the deprivation of years of shortages and high prices, like 1727-28

and 1739-41, but they were sufficiently dependent on sales of
their produce to be much troubled by the unpredictable
markets. They were complaining bitterly. Over-production
meant that 1720-45 were years of very low prices for corn and
wool. Wheat, which farmers usually reckoned to sell for forty
shillings a quarter, was down to twenty-four shillings in 1729
and, after a brief rally to over thirty shillings in 1734-6,
remained stuck in the twenties for most of the years 1737-50.
Wool prices fell by over a third between 1721 and 1740.[17] The
glut of wool meant that graziers were no longer visited by
chapmen from the north, eager to buy. Now the poor farmer
had to take his wool to market in Yorkshire or East Anglia, pay
to warehouse it if he could not sell it or put it into the hands of
factors he did not trust. In the Marsh there had been other
disruptions, intrusions by larger and wealthier farmers from the
Wolds who took marshland pasture to fatten their flocks, but
then abandoned it to inferior farmers as rents increased or they
found that the hardy Scotch cattle could survive on poorer and
cheaper land elsewhere.

More spectacularly, there was disease. Sheep rot was a
constant hazard, but there were severe outbreaks in 1726 and
1730. Most terrifying and devastating for the small grazier was
the cattle plague of 1747. They had watched the progress of this
'disease of horned cattle' as it spread across the country
throughout 1746. Its effects in Lincolnshire were even worse
than expected. In the Fens 10,000 died, so many that the
carcasses lay unburied, their legs at angles to the sky. Elsewhere
whole herds were destroyed. Even those who escaped suffered
because the authorities closed markets and restricted the
movement of all cattle.[18]

These disasters and the prolonged depression were too much
for many small farmers. Already by the late 1720s landlords
were finding it difficult to collect rents. Everywhere the story
was the same. The Whichcot steward told his mistress in
November 1723 that he had not received £12 in rent; in 1728
Mrs Massingberd was told she would have to abate two-thirds of
her rent; on the Monson estates rent arrears exceeded £1,000.[19]
Although landowners preferred to keep tenants if they could
there was a strong temptation to consolidate holdings into the

hands of larger farmers. Many small proprietors simply went to the wall. In Burgh-le-Marsh the number of small occupiers (of twenty-four acres or less) fell from 136 to 100 between 1722 and 1750. On the Monson estate at Owersby the number of tenants fell from seventy-eight in 1729 to fifty-nine in 1744.[20] In the wapentake of Candleshoe the number of smallholders and cottagers (with land worth less than £40 per annum) fell by two-thirds in the eighteenth century and Dr Holderness finds that 'the period in which this change was wrought was 1716 to 1747'.[21]

It is against this background, rather than our retrospective view of a period of stability, that the system of criminal justice in the 1740s should be seen. Those who lived through the prolonged agricultural depression, the Scots' invasion and the cattle plague, thought their age one of anxiety and tumult, with an uncertain future. It was in this context, with limited resources, that they managed to control and even reduce the routine crimes in rural society.

2 RURAL CRIME 1740-80

This chapter describes the crimes which came before the courts in Lindsey. The next section examines the means by which crime was controlled, describing the work of the magistrates, the procedures of the courts and punishments. The underlying theme is that the system was successful because it served the needs of ordinary people and rested on a strong sense of community. It was not a system of oppression .

a) Serious Crime
In general terms serious crime in the eighteenth century might be defined as stealing anything worth more than one shilling, murder, and other very serious violence. Anyone accused of such offences in Lindsey was sent to Lincoln to stand trial at the assizes before the King's judges. Unfortunately the records of Lincoln assizes are lost. All we have are the printed calendars of cases to be heard in the 1770s and chance references in the local and national press. It is slender evidence, but probably enough to draw some conclusions. Table 1 sets out the figures from the calendars.[1]

The first point to make is that offences serious enough to be sent to assizes formed a very small proportion of all crime. During 1771-79, while these eighty-two prisoners were being tried at assizes, the lesser courts of quarter sessions dealt with about 500 criminal cases and many more were heard at petty sessions. The best guess would seem to be that serious crime was less, probably much less, than fifteen per cent of the whole.

TABLE 1
Crimes and Sentences at Lincoln Assizes 1771-79

Estimates of Lindsey cases only.
Source: Printed calendars, LAO Monson 7/91-9

	1	2	3	4	5	6	7	8	9	10
Grand Larceny	21	6	1	4	1	3		1		5
Burglary	18	7	3		1	2	1		1	3
Sheep Stealing	8	3	4							1
Robbery	8	6			2					
Murder	6	3	1					1		1
Stealing Beasts	4		2							2
Rape	3	1						2		
Pickpocket	3	2	1							
Arson	2	1								1
Horse Theft	2	1	1							
Manslaughter	2	2								
Return from Transportation	2	1							1	
Forgery	1	1								
Trespass & Assault	1	1								
Receiving	1				1					
Totals	**82**	**35**	**13**	**4**	**5**	**5**	**1**	**4**	**2**	**13**

Column Headings:

1 Total Cases	2 Not Guilty	3 Death
4 Transportation	5 Imprisonment	6 Burned in the Hand
7 Whipped	8 Bound Over	9 Sent to Army
10 Not Recorded		

The assizes were dominated by serious property crime, which accounted for over sixty per cent of cases heard in the 1770s. Burglary and grand larceny were the most common forms: stealing from private homes, shops, outbuildings and warehouses. The items taken might be valuable, like 'silver spoons' or 'a silver mug'; in 1747 the house of the mayor of Lincoln 'was broken open and robbed of upwards of £200 and the large gold Civic Ring belonging to the City'.[2] However, most of the offences seem to have been committed by petty thieves without much planning. Servants often stole from their employer's private house or shop. Criminal vagrants were always on the look-out for opportunities.

Occasionally, there are hints of a certain professionalism. In April 1743 the shop of Mr John Wharry in Caistor was broken open at night and cloth worth over £60 was stolen, including cotton checks, Leghorn hats, and printed linens. Such items must have been heavy and difficult to conceal. Mr Wharry 'suppos'd the crime was committed by three travelling Trades people'.[3] However, there are few signs of organised crime. In small and scattered rural communities criminal residents were soon discovered, strangers marked, and, above all, the transport system was too primitive to get bulky stolen goods away. Nevertheless, the emphasis on property cases at assizes appears to reflect real concern. It was this type of crime that people were most frightened of, and this fear seems to have increased towards the end of the century. In 1785 the *Stamford Mercury* reported, 'To so daring a pitch has housebreaking become in Lincoln that the inhabitants have entered into a subscription to establish a night watch'.[4]

There were highwaymen. In 1778 'Captain Cox, a notorious highwayman', was hanged at Lincoln after being caught trying to steal a horse from a magistrate's stables at Tathwell. The description given of another robber might have graced a novel: 'Five feet six inches high with brown complexion, had on a light straight-bodied greatcoat, about 38 years of age, rode on a black gelding about 14′ hands, a star on his forehead and a bobtail'.[5] However, he and his accomplice only stole a guinea from a farmer on a lonely road. Most of these criminals were humdrum footpads, some rather desperate and pathetic. The lad who stopped the Peterborough stage in 1774 'had no firearms about him, but made use of a candlestick, instead of a pistol'. The guard drove him off with his blunderbuss, 'lodging two slugs in his forehead'.[6] Travellers were at risk on the lonely roads but footpads never seem to have excited the general consternation aroused by burglars and housebreakers. Rather, they were accepted as one of the hazards of the roads, like floods or pot-holes. Experienced tourists like Viscount Torrington thought it was possible to avoid them altogether if sensible precautions were taken, especially not travelling after dark. He was more troubled by uncontrolled dogs.[7]

Really savage violence in the course of robberies seems to have been rare. In January 1760 the body of a gentleman from Gainsborough was found 'dead, and floating in the cold bath near the town, with two large wounds upon his head, and his pockets rifled of his gold watch and money'. The exceptional nature of this case and the outrage that it caused is demonstrated by the fact that it was reported in the national press, and the crown and the local inhabitants offered a reward of £150 for information leading to a conviction.[8]

There were comparatively few murders and most of them took place within the family. Four of the six cases in the calendars were infanticide: three of mothers killing illegitimate children and the other a man destroying a sixteen-week-old child when he discovered he was not its father.[9] There was one matricide. William Farmery cut his mother's throat 'because she corrected him when he was a little boy'. He admitted the crime was premeditated - he had planned it three years before - but was then driven to make a confession when 'he felt his mother's shade whilst in the Round-house' after his arrest.[10]

As might be expected in a rural area, theft of animals accounted for a significant proportion of crimes tried at assizes, almost twenty per cent. Press reports suggest that many more cases went unsolved, because the animals taken were horses and it was possible to make good an escape on the difficult country roads. Often the animals presented easy targets tethered on commons or kept in small closes. In the five years 1743-47 the *Stamford Mercury* carried twenty-five notices of animals, usually mares or geldings, 'stolen or strayed'. Between 1765 and 1770 there were eighteen such reports. In the same ten years the newspaper recorded just two burglaries and three robberies.

On the limited evidence available about serious crime it does seem possible to draw some conclusions. Assizes were dominated by property crime. While it might be possible to show that the most common crime was theft of animals, the public's greatest fear was of burglary. There was comparatively little cold-blooded violence. The emphasis on property rather than violence was quite different from the pattern revealed by the records of the lesser courts.

b) Assaults

The rest of this chapter is based on the records of quarter sessions for the Lindsey division, 1740-80. The procedures of these courts are discussed below. Here the aim is to describe the different types of crime which came before the bench. Between 1740 and 1780 sessions dealt with about 3,000 incidents; of these nearly 700, or almost one-quarter, were assaults, and this was by far the largest category of offences prosecuted at these courts. Indeed, the figures may be a misleading underestimate. Some of the 3,000 incidents were very trivial, perhaps even artificial, prosecutions of an administrative nature, for example when high constables were encouraged to demonstrate their efficiency by producing exaggerated lists of unlicensed ale-houses in their areas. If such cases are ignored assaults form about half the 'criminal' business before the courts in the 1740s and this figure probably gives a more authentic idea of how the matter appeared to contemporaries.

Two significant conclusions can be drawn from this preponderance of assaults. The first is that the figures agree with other studies which find 'a high level of inter-personal violence' in the eighteenth century. This was a lively, quick-tempered society, in which arguments soon turned to fights. The second arises from the petty nature of many of the cases. 129 of the 700 assaults were punished by small fines of less than one shilling; a further 300 cases were settled by agreement between the parties or binding over to keep the peace. Many of the incidents appear to have been trivial squabbles between poor equals and this is surprising, given the inconvenience and cost of prosecution. The large number of labourers, servants, and poorer people who brought these actions suggests a litigious people who knew the law, took it as part of the fabric of life, and trusted the courts.

As might be expected, many of the petty assaults took place in public houses, but there is no impression of a great mass of drink-related offences as there is in the records of crime in the 1830s and 1840s. Perhaps this was because the eighteenth century tolerated drink more easily: when Viscount Torrington toured Lincolnshire in 1791 he spent more on drink than on food and lodging. He insisted that he could 'carry a good pint of port', regularly 'emptied the bottle' after his evening meal and confessed to being 'a little muddled' when he went to see the Roman antiquities of Lincoln. Such gentlemen were not troubled by a little drunkenness in the lower orders.[11] In 1769 farmer Kelsey suddenly decided to break the pot he had been drinking from; when the landlord's wife objected Kelsey 'struck her in the face with his fist and then took up a table and threw it at her'. The troublesome farmer had to be forcibly ejected, but not without throwing a brick through the window and threatening 'to be revenged on them'. The bench did not consider this serious: Kelsey was fined sixpence.[12]

Rather than discovering a problem of drunkenness, the public house assaults confirm the picture of a good deal of spontaneous violence, of a people quick to anger and resort to fists. In June 1763 Mr Dent, another farmer, went into a public house in Gainsborough and called for a tankard of ale. The girl who served him said he then 'gave her a great deal of ill language', beat her, and fell to so abusing 'everyone who came nigh him' that the landlord threw him out, after a struggle. Questioned, the girl said 'she knows no cause that William Dent had to behave in such a riotous manner ... unless it was that his dog got into her master's pantry and one of the servants gave him a kick'. Perhaps it was sympathy for the dog that led to the dismissal of the prosecution.[13] No doubt many similar brawls are concealed behind the brief statements on the indictments, as when William Odlin was accused of striking Charles Martin 'and breaking his fiddle'.[14]

It would be wrong to suggest that all the assaults were trivial. There were some serious cases: fifty-seven of those convicted were fined more than one shilling; seventy-seven were sent to the house of correction. Some of the 100 bound over to keep the peace were dangerous characters. George Dales of Horncastle was involved in fights, affrays, and stabbings for many years and is last heard of in a warrant to arrest him for assaulting a bailiff. The warrant is marked 'not found'.[15] Robert Bradley, 'alias Dick the Nailer', assaulted high constables, beat up innkeepers' wives, and 'made a great disturbance quarrelling and fighting some butchers' in Barton. He was notorious enough to earn a special note in the sessions minutes and was committed to Lincoln castle.[16]

Not all the disputes were between poor equals: several of the actions for assault were brought by people in authority trying to control the 'Dick the Nailers' of their parish. Edward Cottrell, the Horncastle bailiff, was attacked at least four times in the 1760s.[17] Mr Dixon, a wealthy farmer who later became a magistrate, was set upon by the wife of a labourer because she disagreed with his assessment of the taxes due on her 'windows and lights'.[18] Constables were frequent targets. Jesse Foster, constable of Holton-le-Clay, had to beat off an attacker who tried 'to put a pitchfork through his head'.[19] In three or four cases gamekeepers seem to have been threatened with guns. Schoolmasters were harassed by irate parents. Mr Long, master at Tetney school, was pursued by a local blacksmith, 'who followed him in Town Street ... giving him a great deal of abusive language, and twice knocked him down with his fists'.[20]

A major feature of assault cases is that many of the offences seem to have taken place within homes. There is a strong impression that rural households could be intense and often brutal places. There are thirty-one examples of husbands beating wives, but this underestimates the problem. There are a further 171 cases in which women were victims, but no further details were recorded. Moreover, these prosecutions were usually a last resort, desperate attempts to end violence which had been going on for years. Ann Easton of Luddington told the magistrates that 'On Sunday last and several times before Benjamin Easton her husband has beaten, bruised, and wounded her and put her in fear of her life.'[21] Mrs Major of Ulceby said her husband 'beat her unmercifully'.[22] The magistrates obviously thought there was serious danger when they bound Mr Byron, 'a gentleman', in the large sum of £200 to keep the peace towards his wife.[23] Occasionally there are depositions which give more information about the fearsome domestic battles which eventually drove the wife, or her friends or relations, to prosecute the husband. Sarah Ellis of Flixborough, a carpenter's wife, told the magistrate that her husband

> hath on Sunday and at various times threatened to take away her life. Sometime this last spring when she and her daughter, aged about fourteen, were in bed he carried and put under the bed a furze bush 'all on a blaze', with intent to set her and her daughter with the bed on fire.
>
> A week last Friday he had followed her into the back kitchen with a hay fork in his hand, swearing he would stab her with it and destroy her.[24]

For cold-blooded brutality few exceeded William Paddison of Kirton who 'mayhemmed his wife', (that is, deliberately set out to break her limbs) by throwing her on the ground so that her leg rested over the threshold of a door, and 'stamping on it until it was broken'. He went on to 'attempt to break the other legg, but by the help of some neighbours was happily prevented'.[25]

It may well be that children suffered a good deal, but the ages of victims were rarely given and children could not bring prosecutions against their parents. On one occasion a courageous servant, Rebecca Odling, was beaten by her master when she attempted 'to protect an helpless infant, her master's son, who he had twice knocked down'.[26]

Servants seem to have suffered most of all. Approximately forty actions for assault were brought by servants against masters. Taken together they present a gruesome picture of what servants, many of them little more than children, had to endure. Mary Skellick was apprenticed to a farmer at the age of seven and suffered ten years of 'hard usage' before she ran away.[27] Mr West, a farmer at Willoughton, was accused of 'immoderately beating and wounding his servant, John Smith junior, with a large hazzel stick'.[28] Another servant in husbandry told how his employer's sons had 'three different times' assaulted him by 'taking him by force and violence from off the ground by his ears and legs'.[29] One parish apprentice ran away from her master, a wine merchant, because he had not given her 'sufficient meat and drink' and had 'at different times beaten her in a cruel manner by forcing Chamberley into her mouth and making her swallow it'. Perhaps mercifully, she was returned to the workhouse.[30]

There is a vivid description of a case in Wroot, on the Isle of Axholme, in 1767. One Monday morning, about eight o'clock, a woman returning from her milking saw a servant girl run out of a house with her mistress, Betty Thompson, tearing after her in a rage; 'and when she had overtaken her, she throwed her down upon the ground two several times and beat her with her fist'. The girl escaped to a neighbour's house where the servants bolted the door to protect her against Mrs Thompson, who raved that she would 'murder her if anybody was Murdered in the world'.[31]

People expected servants to be treated badly, and threats of murder were not taken lightly. In 1753 a parish apprentice, 'a dull, lazy boy', disappeared from the house of a baker in Lincoln. It was widely rumoured that he had been murdered by his master. The man was attacked and his trade ruined. Eventually, the boy turned up, sent back to Lincoln by the Billingsgate magistrates, but the master thought it necessary to spend the next three market days standing beside his apprentice on a cart in the cornmarket, shouting, 'Here is Tom - I am innocent'.[32] Not all were as lucky as Tom. On 16 March 1787 William Rawby, a small farmer from Dogdyke, was hanged for the murder of Ann Leary, age thirteen, a parish apprentice. 'The girl's death was caused by ill-usage, her mistress had also beaten her with great severity'.[33]

Finally, let the simple brutality of farmer Shepherd of Willoughton stand as example for many cases. His servant,

Mary Baker, prosecuted him for

> violently beating and abusing her with his foot and
> for striking her with his fist, and punching her
> down and striking her head against the wall, so that
> she was in pain on Sunday of the blows and
> punches which she had received the Wednesday
> before'.[34]

This was the darker side of eighteenth-century vitality. That
spontaneous, lively, 'interpersonal violence' of the public house
and the street, that swift resort to fists, which was so admired by
contemporaries as a sign of vigour, was far less defensible in the
home. There spontaneous violence often meant terrible
beatings and persistent ill-treatment for some wives, some
children and for many servants.

The cruelty of the home and the triviality of many of the
other assaults emphasises the faith which people had in the law.
It was difficult for poor people to prosecute. It was especially
difficult for people like battered wives and servants who might
have to return to the homes of their tormentors. Yet prosecute
they did. Ordinary people, even oppressed people, had enough
knowledge of the system of criminal justice and enough
confidence in it to resort to law. The law was an essential,
fundamental mechanism to regulate the turbulent violence of
their inns, their homes, and their everyday lives. In the
mid-eighteenth century, this tradition was still very strong.

c) Theft

It is perhaps surprising to find that it was Adam Smith who
wrote:

> ... when ... some have great wealth and others
> nothing, it is necessary that the arm of authority
> should be continually stretched forth, and
> permanent laws or regulations made which may
> protect the property of the rich from the inroads
> of the poor ... Laws and governments may be
> considered in this and every case as a

combination of the rich to oppress the poor, and
to preserve to themselves the inequality of the
goods which would otherwise be soon destroyed
by the attacks of the poor ....[35]

The idea that the law upheld the injustice of inequality, that it
was a conspiracy to protect the property of the rich from the
poor, was considerably developed by Marx and has always been
popular among those who wish to see radical change. Some
evidence can be found to support the thesis in the study of crime
in the eighteenth century. This was a very unequal society; the
magistrates were considerable landowners. Above all, the
pre-eminence of property crime at the assizes can be taken to
suggest that the main purpose of those courts was to preserve
the inequitable distribution of wealth.

The previous section has argued that this view is not
supported by the records of quarter sessions; there, the main
business was to settle disputes between poor equals.
Nevertheless there is evidence in the sessions rolls which can be
used to depict the system as fundamentally concerned with the
defence of property.

Theft was the second largest category of crime prosecuted at
sessions, with 450 cases between 1740 and 1780. The forty-five
cases of fraud and sixteen of receiving were closely related and
may be added to make property offences eighteen per cent of all
prosecutions. If the petty administrative matters are ignored,
thefts formed about one-third of the criminal business tried at
sessions.

Further, the magistrates appear to have taken property crime
more seriously than assaults. The records were more carefully
kept and fewer cases were allowed to end informally or by
binding over. Of the 450 accused of theft, 276 went to trial; 160
were convicted and 116 acquitted. It is likely that some of the
other cases were sent to assizes.

Punishments for theft were more severe. Of those convicted
four were fined more than one shilling; seven were sentenced to
imprisonment in the house of correction; eighteen were
transported; 121 suffered the most common punishment, 'to be
flogged until his body be bloody'. What is more, these

punishments seem to have been inflicted for the most trivial offences: when Richard Slingsby of Luddington stole 'beans valued at five pence' he was ordered 'to have twenty lashes on his back'.[36] In this light, the magistrates can be seen as a harsh ruling class protecting their estates by flogging and transporting the lower orders into submission. The argument can be pressed further by looking for examples of honest people driven to steal by hardship or starvation. During the winter of 1776 John Ablard, a labourer,

> ... had no place since May Day last, and was several times in great distress, and went to Boston and Spilsby several times to enlist for a soldier, but could not meet any recruiting parties. As he was coming home from Horncastle market on Thursday night five weeks since, he passed through Mareham-on-the-Hill, and as he went past George Arnall's house (with whom he had lived two years) he saw two pigs in the crew yard, and as he did not know what to do with himself being greatly distressed he determined to steal them.

Entering the yard, he hid in the stable overnight and stole the pigs early on Friday morning. He drove them nearly five miles to Tattershall market, where he sold them for sixteen shillings each, 'throwing in one shilling again for good luck'. On this occasion his luck held, but a month later 'being again in great distress' he stole two more pigs from a yard in Miningsby in the same area. This time he was arrested trying to sell them at the market. He pleaded guilty and was transported for seven years.[37]

Ablard was exceptional. Very few of the accused tried to defend themselves by pleading hunger, perhaps because they knew it would do them little good. One man said he stole a candlestick from an ale-house to sell or pawn 'for meat'. Another was clearly very distressed when caught taking two pecks of meal from some open sacks in a mill. He insisted 'he would not have been guilty of the crime if it had not been for want' and promised 'he would make it up and never be guilty of the same again'.[38]

If such explicit statements are rare, there are several others which imply genuine hardship. One labourer got up at two in the morning to milk a farmer's cow in the field, so that his children might have the milk for breakfast.[39] A woman snatched 'two loaves of wheaten bread' from a stall in Horncastle market. One Friday morning 'about break of the day' in the winter of 1773 a labourer crept up to the rector's barn in Healing and put some wheat into a little bag. As he did so, he was terrified by a cry of 'Holloo'. He immediately dropped the bag, went outside, and confessed 'I am wrong', actions which speak more of an honest man stealing for need than of a criminal.[40]

All but one of these cases took place in winter, but there is no general pattern of an increase of food thefts at that time of the year. However, some particularly bad winters do stand out. The loaves and the meal in the cases above were taken during the famine years of 1765-6. The terrible winter of 1740-1 was the worst. At Epiphany and Easter sessions in 1741 thirteen people were tried for stealing food and one for theft of coals. When men were really hungry they went after sheep, going out on to the Marshes at night in groups of two or three, killing and stripping the sheep, leaving the 'gutts', and carrying home joints of meat to be hidden in earthen jars. Fifteen were killed that winter, as well as four pigs and a goose.[41]

Further justification of theft by hardship can be found if items stolen are classified in a particular way. Of the 412 cases for which precise information survives, fifty-seven were thefts of food, twenty-six of corn, twenty of sheep, thirty-seven of poultry, and four of pigs. Thus it might be said that at least 144 of the total 462 thefts were of food, and this was the largest single category of articles stolen.

Such a classification can be used to argue a case, but it is misleading. By no means all the 'food' was taken to feed hungry families. Consider thefts of geese. The commons, stubbles, and yards of Lindsey supported thousands of geese and they made tempting targets. Elizabeth Dickinson kept an eye open for goslings around the cottages in Hameringham, snapped them up and sold them to contacts in neighbouring villages who asked no questions. Goslings grew rapidly, and soon it was difficult for owners to make positive identification so Dickinson had plied her trade for some time before she was convicted. Mary Corbridge of Haxey worked the same opportunities, stealing the odd gosling from the great commons in the Isle of Axholme and selling them to ale-house keepers.[42]

Like geese, drink is sometimes included in 'food' thefts, but it would be wrong to use these cases as examples of hardship. Charles Shuter, a servant to the vicar of Appleby, regularly stole a bottle of ale from his master's cellar to sell to a woman in the village.[43] These people may have been poor but they and others like them were not driven by desperate want to risk the gallows for a sheep, or to snatch 'two penny loaves' or 'a handful of masseldin'. They stole for gain, and are best thought of simply as thieves.

The 'food' classification is partial. It is much better simply to say that the great bulk of thefts were of petty items, stolen on impulse. There is a technical difficulty here. The formal indictments undervalue the goods because for many years past the valuation had meant the difference between life and death. A man convicted of theft of goods worth more than one shilling was guilty of grand larceny and might suffer death; but if the goods were valued at eleven pence or less he was guilty of petty larceny and would usually escape with a flogging. It is true that by the mid-eighteenth century this distinction was less crucial: grand larceny was usually punishable by transportation and those convicted of petty larceny could suffer the same fate. Nevertheless, at quarter sessions, especially Lindsey quarter sessions, old traditions died slowly, and it was still customary to value many of the items stolen at 'ten pence'. Thus 'a great quantity of wood' in the prosecutor's statement becomes 'three faggots' in the indictment; iron bars which a blacksmith said were worth three shillings and sixpence are valued at ten pence. In one case, silver coins amounting to one shilling and sixpence are valued at ten pence.[44]

Such undervaluation does not shake the general impression given by the depositions of witnesses and prosecutors that the items stolen were small, often ridiculously small. One woman took little pieces of cloth from the shop where she worked to make a quilt. A labourer from Crowle habitually took little pieces of metal, like gate fittings, to sell to a local blacksmith for a few pence. Clothes were favourite targets. It was the practice to put washing out to dry on the hedges around gardens and this proved an irresistible temptation to some of the girls. Rebecca Lee snatched a shift, a shirt, and three caps from a labourer's hedge in Authorpe. Little Ann Pouger was tempted by a red-and-white spotted handkerchief, but was caught when she came back next Monday to steal a cap.[45]

About 215 of the 412 articles stolen might be called petty: 100 small items of clothes, forty-eight farm or workshop implements, twenty-three minor household items, seventeen small pieces of metal, about a dozen small sums of money, and the rest a miscellaneous collection of things from pieces of rope to a Bible and a prayer book. Not only were about half the thefts of trivial items, many of them seem to have been crimes of impulse committed thoughtlessly on the spur of the moment. One girl took a piece of cloth from a shop and then, terrified at what she had done, thrust it into the hands of a friend, telling her to 'burn it or bury it'.[46] Another girl habitually pilfered things, like a small box and a handkerchief from the inn where she worked. Not knowing what to do with them, she hid each one up the chimney. When suspected she rushed to them in panic and just threw them out of the window.[47] One girl spent days trying to decide what to do with a silver spoon she had picked up, clearly marked with the crest of a local magistrate. Eventually she tried to sell it at a market stall in Horncastle, but ran away leaving the spoon when the cutler questioned her.[48] A woman from Haxey tried to hide a stolen chicken by cutting it up and putting it in a pie. However, her friends teased her so much about her 'hen pie' that she dare not collect it from the baker's oven at the end of the day and so was discovered.[49]

The men, who committed three-quarters of the thefts, could be just as silly, especially when drunk. Thomas Foster was arrested 'sat drinking and getting fuddled' and in possession of some stolen shoes and buckles, but he was 'so drunk he could not remember how he got them'.[50] When a Gainsborough wharfinger lost earthenware pots out of some crates, he called the constable and they set off down the Trent in pursuit of a suspect boat. They boarded the vessel to find the pots in the possession of the captain and mate, who were in a sorry state below 'very much in liquor', swearing they 'had no intention to commit a felony' and now 'very much ashamed' of what they had done.[51]

As in the limited information of the assize calendars, there are very few signs of any organised crime in the sessions records. Receivers were always unpopular, because they were regarded as instigators of crime and corruptors of the young. William Germain, a staymaker of Louth, encouraged a thirteen-year-old to steal and embezzle goods for him, in return for regular payments. The boy spent his first earnings on 'a new hat and other necessaries'.[52] There are several other similar cases and the bench took a grave view: two of the sixteen receivers convicted between 1740 and 1780 were sentenced to fourteen years' transportation and five others to be severely flogged. Organised crime was difficult in rural areas simply because the transport system was so primitive that bulky stolen goods could not be moved quickly. Therefore it is probably no coincidence that the one or two examples of thefts which suggest professional planning come towards the end of the period when increasing wealth and improved transport offered more opportunities. In 1776 William Scales confessed that he had made a false key and used it 'at several different times' to 'enter and take wines and brandy out of a warehouse cellar' in Gainsborough. Presumably the stolen items had been shipped down the river.[53]

Thus it needs a particular bias to find class war and a conspiracy to protect property in the records of thefts. Certainly it might be argued that many of the poor had such a low standard of living that they stole tiny items to gain a few pence; and there were times, especially some exceptional winters, when hardship drove some to steal. However, the dominant impression is that thefts reflected the pattern seen in assaults: most of these offences were petty, spontaneous, impulsive crimes. The magistrates acted as if they were chastising silly children rather than controlling a proletariat.

d) Social Crime

It would be wrong, of course, to see everything from the

magistrates' point of view. The idea that the law was an expression of the ideology of the ruling class can be supported in another way. It has been argued that some crime was 'social crime': some offences were legitimate because the poor did not regard them as crimes, even if the landowners' Parliament had made them illegal acts.

It might be possible to see the plunder of wrecks in this way. At times when there were north-east winds the fast tides and shifting sandbanks of Lindsey's coast could be treacherous. Frequently wrecks were left high and dry, especially in the wide sands near Theddlethorpe. There is no suspicion that local people were responsible for the wrecks, but they plundered them with a casual thoroughness which suggests that they did not think it particularly wrong to do so and that such looting was hallowed by long tradition.

All sorts of useful things could be salvaged. William Thickston of Tetney took twelve pounds of treacle, a chamber pot and two dishes from 'a ship lately stranded and cast ashore at North Coates'.[54] Sometimes waggons were driven down to the beach to collect the booty: a Friskney grazier used one to steal a cock-boat washed up on the sands.[55] One memorable night was 7 January 1756, when a ship driven ashore at Somercotes was found to be carrying brandy. Some was taken away in ankers 'slung upon a fork'; some 'in a pail'; some was bottled and 'hid ... among some potato tops'. Unfortunately some was 'mixed with sea water', but the lot they took to widow West in South Somercotes was pronounced 'pretty good' by her son.[56] Many people joined in and by doing so did not become great criminals in the eyes of the community. It all had an atmosphere of *droits de la mare*.

Smuggling is often included in the 'social crime' category because in some parts of the country many of the local people participated, many of the wealthy turned a blind eye (like Parson Woodforde, they were grateful for their cheap brandy) and the revenue laws were seen as unjust attempts to protect special interests. Undoubtedly there was smuggling in Lindsey and some of it had the tacit approval not only of the poor, but of many of the landed gentlemen. It was based on what Adam Smith called 'the cruellest of our revenue laws', the prohibition on the export of wool. This seemed especially unjust in Lindsey, for while domestic prices fell, France offered high returns. It was impossible to police the long Lincolnshire coastline with its many creeks and small inlets, and its swarms of fishing boats which could carry the odd sack of wool out to larger ships. It was believed that few ships left Lincolnshire without one or two sacks of wool tucked away in their holds to make a poor farmer and a sea captain a few shillings in Europe. In 1785 the Yorkshire magistrates were told that ninety tods of wool had been put on board a vessel which sailed from the remote north Lindsey haven of Goxhill for Dunkirk.[57]

Unfortunately, there is no direct evidence of smuggling in the Lindsey sessions records, although there is one interesting case in the roll for Easter 1776. A labourer, Robert Keightly, who lived deep in the Wolds at Goulceby near Horncastle, broke into a warehouse. He stole four gallons of rum, several empty iron-bound casks, a quantity of bottles and some cheese. The quantities suggest that he was no ordinary petty thief; moreover he was cool enough to steal a horse from the stables of a magistrate to commit the crime. It seems he was already known as a suspicious character because the constables went straight to his house and forked over the garden, where they found one of the stolen casks. Keightly really gave himself away when he asked a friend to write a series of letters: one to his father who lived in Market Rasen, urging him to bury any liquor he had received from him; another to a schoolmaster in Faldingworth warning him 'that his house would be searched and he would be strictly examined'. The letter said that the schoolmaster took liquor 'on the understanding it was smuggled'. Another man, Michael Dunn, was instructed 'to utterly deny that he ever carried liquor' for Keightly. Keightly cobbled together a weak alibi for himself but refused to betray any accomplices 'whether he was hanged or transported'. He was transported for seven years, but the depositions suggest that there was more to this case than was ever discovered or recorded. It does not take much imagination to see behind the hints in the evidence some sort of regular network to distribute stolen or smuggled liquor to some quite respectable customers in the Lindsey Wolds.[58]

The social crime *par excellence* was poaching, for the game laws were manifestly unjust and designed to defend the rights of the ruling class. In the eighteenth century only substantial landowners, their eldest sons, or gamekeepers, could take game. The idea behind these peculiar restrictions was that sport was an inducement to the landed gentry to abandon the comforts of the town to carry out their duties as country gentlemen, 'to give freely of their time and fortunes in the service of the community'.[59] Conversely, restricting hunting to the rich was deemed necessary 'to prevent persons of inferior rank, from squandering their time, which their station in life requireth to be more profitably employed'.[60] Thus 'Country gentlemen believed that the game laws were concerned with more than just securing adequate sport for themselves and their friends ... the game laws were measures designed to preserve a stable society.'[61]

If poor countrymen unwilling to accept these restrictions are to be found anywhere surely they will be found in 'famous Lincolnshire' where, according to the song poaching was the 'delight' of many 'on a shiny night in the season of the year'. Literary evidence from disheartened gentlemen at the end of blank days suggests this was indeed the case. One such exasperated outburst is worth quoting at length because it may be the earliest record of an association to prosecute felons in England. This notice appeared in the *Stamford Mercury* in February 1742:

> Whereas there are frequent meetings of gentlemen at the Green Man on Lincoln Heath to hunt, shoot, and take diversions there, and whereas the said gentlemen not only find the said game very scarce thereabouts, but also in the respective lordships adjoining to them, occasioned by the great number of persons not legally qualified who keep greyhounds, nets, and other engines to kill and destroy game. For the preventing thereof it is agreed by the parties who have hereunto subscribed their names as follows:

First, that when any subscriber hereto shall
have information of any person not qualified killing
or destroying any sort of game he shall at the next
meeting at the said Green Man report the same to
the subscribers then present, with the nature of the
game so killed, how, by whom, and the whole
proof that can be made against such offenders,
which subscribers, or the major part of them there
present, shall order and direct in what manner such
offenders shall be prosecuted according to law.

They went on to agree to share the costs of all prosecutions,
and the expenses of 'searching and taking away such guns, dogs,
nets, and other engines' found in the possession of unqualified
persons. Three weeks later they gave more dire warnings:

The JPs who have been acquainted with the said
agreement have determined to punish without
reserve or distinction all offenders against whom
they may have legal proof. Proper informations
will not be wanting, and offenders, for their own
sakes, would do well to observe that the penalty
cannot be remitted as far as the informer is
concerned.[62]

The duke of Ancaster, the lord lieutenant of Lincolnshire,
was a prominent member of the Game Association founded in
1752 to prosecute poachers and dealers and employing 150
people in the task.[63] In the sessions rolls there are certificates
recording the appointments of 240 gamekeepers in Lindsey
between 1748 and 1777.

It all sounds just what we would expect from the fictional
and popular accounts of poaching in Lincolnshire. However,
the reality seems to have been different, although the real
evidence is very difficult to interpret. Even Blackstone found
the statutes for preserving game 'many and various', and 'not a
little obscure and intricate'.[64] In the Lindsey sessions rolls
1740-80 there are only fifty-three cases which might be classified
as poaching; and closer examination reduces the number even

further. Thirty-four of them involved rabbits, six were thefts of fish, two were taking fowls from decoys, and two theft of tame ducks. Technically, these were not offences against the game laws, which applied to wild animals like hares, pheasants, and partridges. These fish, rabbits, and ducks were 'enclosed', the property of the man who owned the land they lived on, and to take them was theft. That leaves just nine cases against the game laws tried at sessions in forty years, all for keeping guns or dogs while unqualified.

It may be that few poachers were tried at sessions, because they could be dealt with in other ways: some might be tried at petty sessions; some might be sent to the court of king's bench. They might be bound over to keep the peace. By chance, we know that at least one Lindsey poacher was treated in this way: in 1769 Thomas Moor appealed against his summary conviction for poaching; no result was recorded, but at the next sessions he was bound over to keep the peace.[65] How many more of the simple records of binding over conceal convictions for poaching it is not possible to say. In his study of the operation of the game laws in Wiltshire, Professor Munsche found that, 'By the late 1730s, few if any violations of the game laws were prosecuted at quarter sessions'.[66]

The most intriguing question is about summary trials. How often did that scene so beloved of popular prints and novels take place: the poacher being tried by the landlord in his own parlour, perhaps on the evidence of only one witness, the gamekeeper? The answer is that we do not know. It was customary for a magistrate to record any summary convictions on a certificate and take that certificate to quarter sessions to be enrolled. The impression from the Lindsey records is that the magistrates were conscientious in this matter, but there are only eighty-two summary conviction certificates in the rolls for the whole period 1740-80 and only four of them record convictions for poaching, while there were forty-five for swearing profane oaths. This disparity may be partly explained by the peculiar fact that the statutes required magistrates to enrol convictions for profane oaths but not those for poaching. However, after 1770 they were compelled to enrol convictions for night poaching. There are none in the Lindsey records.

Professor Munsche found that some poachers were either committed to houses of correction after unrecorded summary conviction, or simply left to rot for a couple of months until discharged at the next quarter sessions. A search of the calendars of prisoners in the houses of correction reveals no such cases in Lindsey. The only Lindsey magistrate who kept 'Justice Books' to record his summary trials was Thomas Dixon of Riby. He lived between two large 'open' villages, next to a large estate well-staffed with gamekeepers and his books cover a later and more troubled part of the century, 1788-98. In those ten years he recorded just one conviction for poaching. Although he did not enrol this at quarter sessions, this evidence does not suggest a high use of summary justice by other magistrates earlier in the century.[67] A flimsy argument might be made using the case of a Kirton-in-Lindsey grocer 'who had in his possession one hare, being unqualified'. He was summarily convicted on the evidence of just one witness, and this might, with some imagination, be interpreted as free use of a routine procedure.[68]

It is possible that dozens of summary convictions went unrecorded, but the balance of the evidence suggests that this is unlikely. Poaching appears to have been much less common in Lindsey than myth and the famous ballad suggest. Certainly it cannot be considered 'social crime', widely sanctioned by the community as a protest against unjust property laws. Indeed, there seems to have been something exceptional about the few poachers who were prosecuted. John Johnson of Lincoln was a violent, almost professional criminal: his wife kept a bawdy house, and when he was tried for poaching he made a serious assault on one of the witnesses.[69] Another poacher was an habitual and violent criminal. He boasted that he had sworn 'to shoot Mr Bull, Mr Banks' gamekeeper', and 'that once he laid in wait for him with a gun loaded with seven or eight bullets, but that Bull went home another way, else he would have shot him'. Eventually, he was transported for burglary.[70] The steward of the Massingberd estate wrote to his master about one of his employees who had taken up poaching:

> I think Robin Showler is not worth your keeping
> for he is varey idle and I fear is given to bad ways,

as I hear gooing out of nits a shooting of Rabits and
hath taken Horses out of nits hee sildom ever is to
be found at nite and sildom coms to super.
Scremby oficers fetcht him last week with a warant
and maid him marey a wench he had a Child by. [71]

The reckless yet determined criminality of these men makes
them exceptional. It is almost as if they were deliberately
stepping outside the law, and in this they were rejecting, not
representing, the community in which they lived. The ordinary
man who liked to go out 'with a ferret in his bosom' went after
rabbits and if he went in the growing season the farmer would
not mind too much. Thirty-four of the 'poaching' cases were
prosecuted during winter, between November and January,
when farmers were more nervous about theft and trespass of all
kinds. If the men wanted to enrich a poor winter diet the
enclosed rabbits and poultry offered much easier targets than
wild pheasants. If they were really starving, as in 1740-1, they
went after sheep.

In the eighteenth century the Lindsey gentlemen were
concerned with the preservation of game, but often it was the
overindulgence of qualified guns that they feared as much,
perhaps more, than the poacher. 'It is usual for a Man who
loves Country Sports to preserve the Game on his own
Grounds, and divert himself upon those that belong to his
Neighbours', wrote Addison.[72] Shooting was popular, and there
was strong pressure on the gentry to grant rights to tenants and
friends. At least one third of the 240 gamekeepers appointed
between 1740 and 1780 were clergy, tenants, and other
sportsmen for whom the gamekeeper's certificate was simply a
licence to shoot. When the famous hunter Mr Chaplin was
disappointed by a blank day because the game on his manors
had been 'greatly destroyed', he resorted to the usual notice in
the *Stamford Mercury*. Before offering rewards for information
about poachers, the first half of the notice 'requested' qualified
persons not to kill or course hares except on certain days.[73]

Certainly this attitude changed towards the end of the
century, after enclosure and the French Revolution, but in the
1740s and 1750s there was little of the class war in poaching.

The threat to stocks of game came more from qualified
sportsmen than from poachers; the protests of the gentry were
prompted by blank days rather than fear of the lower orders; the
poachers were often exceptional, deviant men, rather than
representatives of the poor; and poaching was far less common
than might be expected. It makes a doubtful case for 'social
crime'.

e) The Economic Community
In eighteenth-century rural England there was a powerful idea
that economic activity should be subject to the community,
morality, and the law. Partly this was because many villages still
farmed their land by strips in open fields. First, this created a
sense of community because the village was the unit of
economic production. Second, and more simply, the complex
farming of the open fields and commons could not be carried on
without strong communal organisation. Regulation was
essential, fundamental, if the system was to operate at all. Such
traditions were ancient, deeply embedded in people's beliefs. In
the past, local farming customs had been administered by the
manor courts, where the power lay with the jury of those who
held land of the manor. Some of these courts were still
operating in Lindsey in the eighteenth century. At Crowle
substantial fines of anything between one and five shillings were
being imposed on neighbours who obstructed watercourses, did
not clean their drains, did not mend their fences, or allowed
their cattle to wander over others' crops. One inhabitant was
fined 'for discovering the Secrets of his Fellow Jurors'; another
for 'indecently using Tobacco and otherwise misbehaving
himself to the rest of his fellow jurors'.[74]
    However, by 1740 the manor courts had disappeared, or
ceased to be effective in many villages and therefore regulation
of farming passed to the court of quarter sessions. There are
over 200 farming offences in the sessions rolls 1740-80, but this
must be only the tip of the iceberg: the rather distant and
imposing quarter sessions was a comparatively expensive and
formal way of settling interminable petty open-field disputes.
The ignorant, inconsiderate, or lazy farmer probably had years
of remonstrance and complaint before his exasperated

neighbours took him before the justices. A farmer at Usselby was indicted for allowing his cattle to wander on the common fields 'on the first of July 1749 and at forty other times'.[75]

Many of the cases arose when a farmer did not maintain his section of the fences around his closes or his portion of the open fields and animals got in amongst the growing crops. Typical, and a good example of the local procedure, was a case at Tumby. There a farmer called William Shepherd persistently refused to maintain his fence, so his animals wandered all over the corn. The local field jury of the other farmers who worked the land 'viewed the fence, and judged it proper that he should be indicted'. This pronouncement was intended as a warning and they delayed proceedings, hoping Shepherd would mend his fence. When he did not, as a further warning, the pindar 'pind his animals several times', but then released them without charging the customary fine. However, on the last occasion Shepherd demonstrated his violent contempt for communal restraints by rescuing his animals by force: 'throwing down the pindship, he went and took the cattle out of the fould'. It was only at this point that the field jury decided to go to law and they asked the parish constable to present, that is bring proceedings against, Shepherd at the next sessions.[76] No doubt such repeated warnings and use of communal agencies like the field juries, pindars, and constables preceded many of the appearances at sessions.

Among tough farmers in small communities, such disputes might create great bitterness over time and occasionally matters got out of hand. The Massingberd steward wrote to his master about two of the tenants on the estate:

> Mr Ward and Bainton Hath had Sum Deference. Bainton had eight best goot up on Mr Ward's tornaps. Mr Ward Set his Dogs at them and Drufe them to Brinkhill town side and then Mr Ward opend the gate and let them into the town a mongest sum best that had the Distemper. At that time Bainton went to Mr Bateman to know what he must Do about them.

Mr Bateman, the magistrate, arranged an agreement and compromise between them, but as the steward wrote, 'I wish they may keep it so, it hath cawsed a grate Dell of talk about us, and Mr Ward is much blamed for Doing such a Mad pees of work.'[77]

Perhaps there was something in that conventional justification for enclosure: that it would enable 'frequent Trespasses and Disputes among the several Proprietors to be prevented'.[78] Usually the disputes were kept within reasonable bounds and were settled by fines of sixpence or a shilling, the same penalties as those inflicted by Crowle manor court. Stiffer punishments were very rare, but in 1749 two farmers were fined £10 and sent to the castle at Lincoln 'until payment' for pound breach, and a grazier was fined £10 for moving cattle during the cattle plague of 1747.[79]

The rest of the farming cases were such matters as 'failing to maintain dykes', 'ploughing up the town's ground' and 'blocking the road with a cart of manure'. Several refer to the commons. John Teesdale was fined twopence because 'he did for one month put six sheep on Hogsthorpe Common with no right to common.' William Hotchin junior, of West Keal, 'did erect a cottage for himself and family on the waste, occupied the house and manured four acres of ground there'.[80]

  The other major area of local economic life which came under the control of the courts was relationships between masters and servants. Many servants were hired by the year and lived in their employer's home, often in rather intense and overcrowded conditions. When difficulties arose the contracts were enforced by the courts. There are only twenty such cases in the sessions records, but other evidence suggests that the problem was much larger: many of the assaults arose out of disputes between master and servant, and Mr Dixon's Justice Books, the only surviving accurate records of summary justice, show that half his work, forty cases in ten years, was settling master and servant disputes.

On the masters' side the usual complaints were that the servant, having accepted the fastening penny and agreed the contract, then disliked the accommodation, the master or mistress, or had a different assessment of what the work required. Rebecca Green of Irby, having been hired for the year, was accused of 'several misdemeanors' in 'neglecting her work and refusing to obey the reasonable commands of her master'. Eventually, as was common, she 'absented herself' from her master's service. The law seemed weighted on the employers' side and punishments were harsh. No shilling or sixpenny fines in these cases: the standard punishment for girls like Rebecca Green was three months in the house of correction.[81]

However, the law did offer protection for the servants too. One third of the master and servant prosecutions were brought by servants against their employers, usually for 'non-payment of wages'. A staymaker from Gainsborough took his master to the sessions because he 'owed him 19s. 5d. wages and keeps his clothes'.[82] John Lyon, a servant in husbandry, constantly disagreed with his employer. After six months they agreed to part, but the master refused to pay any wages. Lyon immediately went to see the local justice, Mr Whichcot, who issued a warrant to the constable to summon the farmer to appear before him 'this afternoon'. He was then ordered to pay the wages. The summons 'to show why wages not paid' was a printed form and Whichcot had marked it 'No. 47', suggesting that such cases were far more common than the few which reached sessions.[83]

The willingness of servants to use the courts to prosecute their employers is another instance of the poor being aware of their rights and of their confidence in the legal system. It must have been a considerable undertaking for a poor servant to bring proceedings against an employer to whom they were bound for a year, who might be a tenant of the local justice and in whose house they might still have to live for many months.

This sense of justice, and that economic life should be subject to law and morality, went much further than arbitration between master and servant and regulation of the open fields. There was a general belief in some sort of 'moral economy': that economic affairs should be conducted according to certain standards of decency and morality; the interests of the community must always be considered; tradesmen and middlemen should take just returns and no more; there was a just price for goods. If people would not observe these concepts then society, through the law and the courts, must force them to do so. Economic selfishness and immorality must be controlled in the same way as any other form of anti-social behaviour. A pamphlet of 1768, discussing a farmer's claim to sell his corn to his own best advantage, the right of each person 'to do as he liked with his own', argued that,

> It cannot then be said to be the liberty of a citizen, or of anyone who lives under the protection of any community; it is rather the liberty of a savage; therefore he who avails himself thereof, deserves not that protection the power of Society affords.[84]

The idea of 'free enterprise', that each individual vigorously pursuing his own economic interests would, by some 'invisible hand', bring prosperity to all, would have seemed outrageous to most ordinary country people in the eighteenth century. No doubt this was because their wider horizons were limited; they had no understanding of great economic forces; they did not perceive the 'hidden hand'. They saw their neighbours living close to the breadline in their small communities and supplied by their local markets; the social and personal consequences of economic actions were keenly felt and they tended to assume that economic changes must have local, personal, causes.

There was a strong concept of the 'just price'. Of course they realised that prices might rise or fall, depending on the harvests, and a steady, long-term trend in prices could be explained. But generally prices were more stable then and people had a rather static idea of what they should be: the standard labourer's wage was eightpence a day for many years. When the shoemakers of the county of Lincoln were compelled to increase prices in 1767 they thought it worthwhile, perhaps necessary, to place a large advertisement in the local newspaper explaining that the increases were due to 'the extreme high price of leather and the great losses they have sustained' and insisting that they were making a 'proportioned advance' in prices.[85]

In this atmosphere it was natural to expect that the law, through the magistrates, would control prices. The bench at quarter sessions set annually the rates which might be charged by common carriers, and the tolls of some turnpiked roads.[86] The keeper of the ferry across the Trent at Owston was twice presented by the grand jury for 'extortion' in 'taking too much fee'.[87]   The most important such regulation by the magistrates was to set the Assize of Bread. This controlled the weight and price of the most essential foodstuff, on which poor families often spent three-quarters of their income. In 1754 Humphrey Brown of Alford, baker, was fined because he 'did bake, make, and expose for sale one sixpenny loaf' which was underweight.[88] Although this was the only such prosecution it is clear that the Assize was still maintained vigorously in the 1770s. The sessions minutes record a meeting between the magistrates and the bakers to set the rates, 'with which the Bakers were at first dissatisfied'. One thousand forms 'relative to the Assize of Bread' were ordered to be printed, and the Clerks of the Market, who were also 'weighers and distributors of the Assize', were instructed to make returns to the justices of 'the Average Price of Corn once every fortnight'.[89]

Markets were also controlled by the magistrates. Again people saw markets in local terms: farmers and producers should take their goods to market and offer them for sale openly so that they might reach a just price. There was considerable suspicion of dealers and merchants. It was understood that prices might rise or fall according to the harvest and that a dealer who collected goods together and transported them or distributed them might take a just return for his trouble, but certain practices were forbidden. It was illegal to 'engross or forestall', that is to make private agreements to buy or sell before coming to market; it was illegal to 'regrate', to buy goods in one market to sell again in another for a higher price. There are fifteen offences against these laws in the sessions records. Fairly typical was Sarah Tonge of Gainsborough, who in 1775

> did obtain and get into her hands two threepenny household loaves of bread and two sixpenny household loaves of bread for one shilling and fourpence, the said loaves being brought to market to be sold, and afterwards in the same market did

unlawfully regrate the said loaves and sell the same
at one shilling and sixpence.[90]

Sometimes the bigger dealers were prosecuted. In 1740,
William Spark of Barton 'did engross and gett into his hands by
buying of and from Christopher Hildyard 88 acres of Wheat,
Rye, Barley and Beans with intent to sell the same again'.[91]

In the 1740s such cases were some of the last offences to be
dealt with by presentment by the parish constable, emphasising
that they were crimes against the community. In 1742 the
constable of Brigg presented four grocers 'for buying butter and
other things in our market to sell again to the great prejudice of
the inhabitants and others, and for which we desire they may be
indicted'. Apparently the case led to a row between stallholders
and the public, because an action for assault arose out of it.[92]
Such incidents could quickly turn into minor food riots: at
Caistor market in 1757 six people were charged that 'they did
take, spoil, and throw away ... twenty pounds of butter'.[93]

The market laws were especially likely to be invoked if prices
rose suddenly or to an excessive degree. Then it was suspected
that some human agency, some sharp practice by middlemen,
must be responsible. In 1766 a poor harvest was followed by a
harsh winter (Epiphany sessions at Caistor was postponed 'by
reason of the depth of snow and inclemency of the weather') and
there were widespread food shortages and riots. The *Stamford
Mercury* was full of reports of the disturbances, particularly in
the neighbouring counties of Nottinghamshire, Leicestershire,
and Norfolk. In this atmosphere the attitude of the authorities is
an interesting reflection of economic ideas. The government
and magistrates might simply have warned with threats against
the consequences of violence. They chose a quite different
policy, supporting the public belief that the shortages were
exacerbated by the selfishness or sharp practice of some of the
farmers and dealers. In May 1766 the *Mercury* reported that
near Boston

> a gentleman had lodged an information against a
> forestaller who had contrary to law engrossed a
> number of lambs and is now in prosecution for the

same. We are likewise informed enquiries are out
after some other persons who have been frequently
guilty of the like offence.[94]

In October the Stamford magistrates took into consideration
'His most generous Majesty's proclamation for putting into
execution the laws against forestalling, regrating and enclosing'.
They resolved that 'Strict attention and obedience be paid to the
regulations, and ordered that Clerks of the Market, searchers of
corn markets and all other constables be vigilant'. A fortnight
later the royal proclamation 'was read in the cornmarket, and
upwards of one thousand copies ... printed ... and dispensed
amongst the country people'.[95]

Few of those who read or heard the proclamation realised
that this was one of the last occasions on which the old
communal regulations would be enforced in an attempt to deal
with famine and major riots. Most ordinary people still
expected communal justice in farming and in food supply to be
upheld by the law, acting through the manor courts, the field
juries, the magistrates and the sessions.

f) Sexual Offences
Some of the most numerous documents in the sessions rolls are
bastardy bonds, 309 of them between 1740 and 1780. When a
single woman became pregnant it was an offence against the
community and the parish authorities were soon involved. It
should be stressed that the concern was economic, not moral.
The overseers and churchwardens of the parish wanted to know
who was going to pay to support the child and make sure that
the rate-payers did not suffer. It was no use the girl or her
parents insisting they would keep the child; the overseers wanted
more concrete guarantees. Accordingly, as soon as a single girl
was seen to be pregnant she was carried before the local
magistrate to explain how she came to be with child and to say
who the father was. Silence meant commitment to the house of
correction. Usually the girl confessed and the magistrate issued
a warrant to the constable to arrest the father. Both parents
were then required to enter into a bond to support the child.
The usual conditions were that the father was bound in the sum

of £40, and to find two other sureties or £20; he was to pay the midwife and any other fees, perhaps a guinea or two; and thereafter he was to pay one shilling and sixpence each week to keep the child. The mother was to pay sixpence. The bond was then enrolled at the next quarter sessions.

It is easy to find harshness in the overseers' treatment of young girls who must often have been distressed, but the cost of supporting an illegitimate child could be a serious matter for a small farming community. The whole process is accurately recorded by the accounts of the overseer of Scooter. When Elizabeth Walker asserted that John Baxter was the father of her child the constable set off to get a warrant from the local magistrate, who lived at Thonock:

A journey for warrant unto Thonock	2s.	0d.
Pd for warrant at Thonock	2s.	0d.
Pd unto two men for attending Baxter at Scotter all night	2s.	0d.
Victuals and drink to the attendants & Baxter	5s.	0d.
A horse for Baxter to the Justice at Gainsboro	1s.	6d.
One for myself at the same time	1s.	6d.

Next there was the trip to Caistor for the sessions, more expensive than usual because there was heavy snow that January:

A journey to Caistor, there confined by distress of weather until the 17th	8s.	0d.
For my horse and self charges on the journey	16s.	0d.

Finally, there were the costs of the birth:

Pd for fetching the midwife and carrying home again	1s.	0d.
Pd unto the midwife for executing her office	2s.	6d.
Pd unto a man for fetching the apothecary to the child	4s.	0d.
The apothecary's bill	4s.	6d.
Pd Elizabeth Walker in time of her month £1	0s.	0d.

What with one or two other journeys and incidental expenses, the full bill was £4 13s. 0d.[96]

As for the alleged fathers, the sudden appearance of a constable with a warrant was not the best way to learn the glad tidings of impending paternity, and their reactions were unpredictable. A sailor at Gainsborough gathered his crewmates and threatened to throw the constable overboard; a man from Sturton 'went up to London with a drove of beasts and has not been heard of since'; some had to be committed to the house of correction until they agreed to be bound to pay. There was always the possibility of marriage and there are one or two notes from local curates certifying that they have married prospective parents 'according to law'. Probably most agreed to pay, and hoped it would not be for long. A recent study of the Gainsborough registers for the last years of the eighteenth century found that 'None of the 94 bastards recorded in the registers survived infancy'. In the sessions rolls the Garthorpe overseers added this to their accounts for a birth: 'the child ... died a fortnight and three days after it was born'.[97]

The mothers' statements give some information about how they came to be pregnant. There is little evidence of that childish spontaneity found in the assault and theft cases. It is rare to find the frolic in the hay field, although Elizabeth Hollandtrick told the magistrate that she had conceived her child 'in a piece of ground ... called Dovecoat Close where she was helping John Markham to make hay, and he laid her down under a haycock'. However, Miss Hollandtrick also confessed 'that several other men had carnal knowledge of her about two years since and upwards', and in this, too, she seems to have been exceptional.[98]

Many of the cases involve servant girls, confirming the unpleasant impression of servant life given by the records of assaults. Young girls usually moved to a neighbouring village when they went into service. Often away from home for the first time, living in overcrowded houses, intimidated by the older men, they were at risk. Sometimes it was the master: Ann Baldwick said her farmer employer 'had carnal knowledge of her several times, and especially when the clock struck one on Christmas Eve and from that time on for several times after, so long as she continued to be his servant, namely until the Friday after May last'.[99] Sometimes it was the son: Mary Hardy said that young Joseph Saunderson 'frequently lay with her from Midsummer to Martinmas in his father's house at Winterton'.[100] Most often, it was a fellow servant. A number of women explained that another servant, usually an older man, had 'persuaded her to lett him lye with her'. Frequently, 'weedlings and promises of marriage' are mentioned and often the statements end, 'no other person hath had carnal knowledge of her since'.[101] The dominant theme is of chaste but vulnerable young women seduced by older servants. Many of the depositions are pathetic, even tragic, ending with the illiterate's 'her mark'.

Not much evidence of sexual violence remains because rape cases would normally be sent to assizes, but there are five assault cases which mention attempts to 'rape', 'ravish and beat', or 'carnally know'. One may have been an employer attacking a servant girl, when a farmer called Dalton was convicted of attempting to rape a servant 'an infant under twenty one'.[102] The magistrates do not seem to have thought the case serious: Dalton was fined half a crown; another man convicted of 'ravishing and beating' was fined a shilling. Only one man from the five cases was sent to the house of correction. He had attacked a girl, 'putting her in bodily fear by pulling up her clothes in a shameful manner'.[103]

There is some evidence of organised vice, but prosecutions were rare because it was probably dangerous for a private individual to bring a successful action against a disorderly house. Usually it was left to the constables, or on one occasion a clergyman, to assume the task. Between 1740 and 1780 there were fifteen prosecutions for keeping brothels: four in Lincoln, four in Gainsborough, and two in Barton. The rest were in villages: Reepham, Wainfleet All Saints, High Toynton, and Langworth.

The constables of Lincoln give us some account of one of these houses:

> They believe Elizabeth Mumby, whose husband is
> in the militia and has long been absent from her,

keeps a common bawdy house ... for that several complaints have lately been made against her for entertaining common prostitutes and other lewd and disorderly persons, and allowing ... great disorders in her house.

One of the complainants, an indignant neighbour, gave a more colourful description of the premises. He asserted that

he hath within the last six months last past seen several men in the very Act of fornication or adultery with the women in the said Elizabeth Mumby's dwelling house ..., and that Elizabeth Mumby constantly entertains common prostitutes ... at all hours of the night and day, and frequently invites and entices men into the said house to accompany with her and other lewd women, and that the disorders lately committed there is a publick nuisance to the neighbourhood.[104]

The constables raided another bawdy house in the Bail of Lincoln in 1746. Inside they found: Elizabeth Clark from Newcastle, who claimed to be 'only drinking a pint of ale, and that she has trevelled selling pedlar'd goods'; Sarah Prime, 'now going to Gainsborough market with Elizabeth Clark'; Susannah Dodson, 'a woman of evil fame'; and Elizabeth Bland from Sheffield, who frankly admitted 'that two men have lately had carnal knowledge of her body in the said house'. Unfortunately, the constables picked the wrong night, for there were a number of soldiers in the house and they resented the interruption to their evening's entertainment. A brisk riot developed in which a mob, 'riotously and tumultuously assembled', caused 'great disturbance and terror' in the town, and smashed all the windows in the constable's house. A drunken labourer staggered through the tumult, offering sixpence 'to any person that would tell the Justice he was a fool'.[105]

Finally, there are one or two cases of homosexuality. Two men from Long Owersby were bound to answer a charge of committing 'an act of sodomy'.[106] Such acts were capital offences, and the risk of blackmail was great. A wheelwright from Alford was tried for 'sending a letter to Israel Close, clerk, threatening to accuse him of the most horrible and detestable crime called buggery with a view to extort gain'.[107]

The main conclusions to be drawn from the sessions records about sexual offences seem to be: that the concern was economic, not moral; that many illegitimate births were by servant girls, confirming the unpleasant picture of servant life given elsewhere in the records; and that there were some brothels, especially, as might be expected, in the larger towns. In most cases the proceedings were initiated not by private individuals but by the parish authorities, the overseers or the constables.

g) Vagrants

Of all the documents in the quarter sessions rolls, the richest and most varied are the depositions of 'rogues and vagabonds found wandering and begging' in villages and towns throughout the county. There are 338 of them from 1740 to 1780, and they offer fascinating biographies of some of the poorest people of the eighteenth century. Again, the motive for this thorough documentation was economic. The arrival of a vagrant caused immediate concern, for even a short stay might prove expensive for the parish. Waddingham's officers were caught when a soldier's wife gave birth to a child in their village in 1743. What with the midwife's charges for 'two nights and one day' in labour, 'blankitts, victuals, soap and cannels', the clerk's fee for the churching and 'crissing' , and a gift of 2s. 6d. 'when she went away', the total bill came to £1 14s. 7d.[108]

The apparent generosity of the gift reveals the fear that haunted parish authorities. Paupers were the responsibility of the parish in which they had settlement. Often this was the parish in which they were born, but settlement might also be gained by serving an apprenticeship, marriage, employment, or ownership of property. The overseers were terrified in case any vagrant managed to establish settlement in their village because he might then become 'chargeable' to the parish for ever. Thus as soon as a vagrant appeared in a village he was whisked off to the magistrate to be thoroughly examined to find out where he had settlement and which parish was responsible for him. This done, the vagrant was issued with a pass, entitling him to support on his journey home. The constable then took him to the parish boundary and delivered him into the hands of the next constable, who 'passed' him on. Sometimes informal procedures were used. The woman who gave birth in Waddingham was simply paid to go away.

It was not always so simple. Fear of chargeability often led the authorities to callous treatment of vagrants. Just before Easter, 1766, a woman wandered into the village of Wainfleet All Saints. She was ill, and carrying a nine-month-old child. The constable immediately passed her on to the neighbouring parish of Croft. There, later that night, she died. Wishing to limit their expenses to a pauper funeral Croft overseers sent the child back to Wainfleet insisting he was their responsibility.[109]

Something of a record was established in 1742 when the overseers of Fillingham brought an action against no fewer than seven parishes for removing 'a poor travelling woman bigg with child ... when she was not in a condition fit to be removed'. The court proceedings revealed that in an advanced state of pregnancy, perhaps with labour imminent or begun, the constables had hustled this woman across Burton, South Carlton, North Carlton, Scampton, Aysthorpe, Brattleby, and Cameringham. This journey of eight miles only ended in Fillingham because the woman gave birth. And of course, Fillingham's court action was not prompted by compassion; it was simply that if they could prove the woman had been wrongly removed she and her child would become the problem of Lincoln or one of the intervening parishes, not theirs.[110]

But the accolade for thick-skinned ingenuity must go to the churchwardens and overseers of Kelstern. They were supporting Elizabeth Lyon, spinster, 'she being lame'. No doubt the expenses were a considerable burden for a small parish. Therefore the appearance of Thomas Ogle, 'a poor man legally settled in North Willingham', proved too great a temptation for the calculating officers. 'They did conspire and agree to give the said Elizabeth for the use of ... Thomas Ogle', and offered him four guineas if he would marry her. He agreed to the bargain. They were married 'in the parish church of

Kelstern the next day' and then immediately passed to North Willingham. The reaction of the overseers there may be imagined. They brought an action for unjust removal, protesting at 'the great expense of supporting Thomas Ogle and his wife'.[111]

There seem to have been a great number of people on the road and vagrants must have been a much more common sight in the villages than they are today. People were frightened of them. Vagrants were often dirty; they begged in the streets and tapped at back doors, and could be intimidating. Mrs Skelton of Wragby complained that a beggar in ragged soldier's dress was 'lodged in a barn' near her house and that his demands for relief were 'threatening her and putting her children in fear of some bodily harm'.[112] Others were suspicious, always on the look-out for something to steal. One Saturday afternoon in 1778 a small gang of vagrants came to Belton. There were two young women, two men and three children, leading a string of donkeys. They steadily 'worked' the town, 'wandering and begging'. One of the women went into a blacksmith's shop, 'stayed a short time', but apparently bought nothing. In fact she pilfered two horseshoes. The blacksmith, the constables and some parishioners went after them and, in the panniers carried by the donkeys, found 'several bundles containing goods stolen by the gang'.[113]

Deception was common. Some of the vagrants carried large and impressive documents issued by magistrates, explaining that they had suffered some personal disaster, and were therefore licensed to beg. This procedure was widely abused. John Slater 'travelled England with a a false paper pretending that he had lost £630 by fire'.[114] John Moor claimed to have been a soldier 'wounded at Preston Pans', but his companion confessed that he was really 'a lusty man in a blue coat who begged as a dumb man but who spoke well enough to him'.[115]

For many village people there was something alien, almost magical, about some of the vagrants. They were unsettled, unattached, 'wandering about', in a world bound by the demands of making a hard living, tied by families, masters and contracts of service. No wonder many vagrants made money by telling fortunes. They were fond of tall tales, mixtures of fact and

fantasy which went down well in village inns.   One common
theme was America: several vagrants claimed links with America,
or to have spent some time there and this easily expanded to
include the ownership of huge estates.   Thomas Healey, arrested
for begging in the Bail of Lincoln, told the magistrate that he had
been born at 'Burlington on the Delaware river near
Philadelphia, and had served in the English navy as a common
sailor eighteen years and two years in the artillery as a soldier'.
He had been discharged at Chatham eleven years ago and had a
pension of £12 per annum.   Indeed, he was just on his way to
collect his pension and, he went on, 'he had 300 acres of land in
New Jersey ... and he intends to go to New Jersey as soon as he
... can raise money for his passage there'.   He was delayed,
because the magistrate sent him to the house of correction.[116]

Three young men, who gathered a crowd in Louth in
November 1750, gave the best version of another common
romance.   They were sailors, just returned from the
Mediterranean, where their merchant vessel had been captured
by Turkish pirates after 'a battle with two shebecks of two great
guns forward, besides swivels and pottereros', the 'smart
engagement' lasting 'five-and-a-half hour glasses'.   They were
eventually 'forced to yield after twenty-one men were killed and
wounded and only eleven left whole'.   The leader of the Louth
group, a young man called Thompson, was 'cut with a scimitar
across the arm'.   They were then thrown together in prison at
'Sallee' where they underwent many hardships and adventures.
Thompson was 'hung up by his arms for fifteen minutes on
tenter hooks at the market cross on a beam like a butcher's
beam across the market house'.   They were set to work as slaves,
'carrying lime and water', 'plowing the vineyards' and 'drawing
stones from the quarry'.   After a year they tried to escape 'by
cutting a galley out of the old Mole close by Sally in the night
time and were out at sea all night, but for want of a compass
they came upon their shore again, when the Rovers sent two
galleys to take them in again'.   They were condemned to the
galleys, 'chained four to an oar', cruising the Mediterranean 'to
fight against the Christians', until they were rescued by two
Maltese men-of-war and taken to Leghorne, from where they
made their way home.   It was a tale worthy of Defoe; indeed, as

with the tales of America, it was so reminiscent of some of that author's work that one wonders if there was any relationship between the two. The magistrates did not believe it; Thompson and his friends were packed off to the house of correction.[117]

Of the ordinary vagrants, their reasons for being on the road were so varied that it is difficult to generalise, but one or two themes stand out. Some were simply poor people for whom any journey was a hazardous undertaking. Sarah Smith 'had come from Lancashire to see a sister at Grimsby, but found she was dead, and being short of money was obliged to beg her way home'.[118] The hundreds of harvest workers who came to Lincolnshire in the summer were normally allowed to pass freely unless they fell ill. Robert Brearly, aged twenty-two, 'having been at harvest work in the Fens' was 'very much afflicted with the ague and feaver' rendering him 'unable to travel home without assistance'.[119]

Many had been wanderers from an early age. George Fearon told Justice Whichcot in 1774 that he 'was born in the old town of Aberdeen left it about 1740 and has been strolling about the kingdom ever since'.[120] James Gibbs had been abandoned by his parents at the age of five and had been a vagrant ever since. When he was arrested in Louth in 1743 he was sixty-one.[121] Just starting on a similar career was Sam Squire, aged twelve, who said he 'was born a bastard, but does not know in what place and has no account of his father'. He had 'wandered about the country with his mother begging their bread ever since he can remember, till her death, since which time he has wandered by himself'.[122]

Margaret Foster was one of several 'fallen women' in the rolls. She had been born in London and her first job had been as a servant in the 'Red Lion' inn, Barnet. Here she was tempted by Robert Adams, a cordwainer, who 'pretended courtship ... and promised to marry her'. They ran away together and 'travelled several months' until they reached Edinburgh. There she 'found she was with child', and Adams 'left her ... and enlisted for soldier'. Margaret now tried to make her way home, but 'she had few or no clothes left' and 'nothing to support herself but two shillings she had given her at Caistor'. Her child, a daughter, was born in Market Rasen.[123]

William Crabtree may serve as the example of the huge class of what might be called young men who could not settle. Aged twenty-one in 1776, he had been born at Belton. Perhaps his parents were unwilling to support him for at the age of six he had been apprenticed to a local farmer. In all he lived with three farmers until he was about thirteen, when he went as 'a labourer day-to-day' thrashing out corn. After five months of this he 'went into Yorkshire and ship'd himself for a voyage to Davis's Straight'. On return he worked as a navvy on the Market Weighton canal 'and then joined company with Thomas Hewson, wandering and travelling the country showing tricks with cups and balls'.[124]

One of the clearest impressions is how many of the vagrants claimed some association with the armed services. These were the years of the great wars with France and people who had been caught up in them formed a large contingent of the travellers. There were soldiers' wives like Lucy Axtill, who said she had been married to 'Loftus Axtill, a common soldier in General Tatler's Regiment of Foot, and was killed at the battle of Fontenoy'.[125] Typical of the soldiers was Matthew White. Aged 'about fifty' in 1769, he had been 'born in the army in French Flanders' and had served thirty-four years, eventually being discharged from Captain Charles Long's Company of the 73rd Regiment of Foot in 1760. Since then he had travelled the country 'sometimes at harvest work, at other times a petty chapman selling small wares and sometimes asking charity'. He had married, and when he was arrested for begging in Fiskerton he had with him his wife Jane and two children under seven.[126]

One of the many old Royal Navy sailors taken up for vagrancy was Richard Cross. He had begun life as a baker's apprentice, but 'in the last war was pressed into His Majesty's ship *Lennox*, commanded by Admiral Cornish', and 'served eight years as a baker on board'. After the end of the war, in 1764, he had been paid off and 'maintained himself by buying rags and selling pins, needles, laces, nets, and petty chapman's wares'. Like the soldier, he had married, but there were no children.[127]

Perhaps it is just possible to relate changes in the numbers of vagrants to the wars. There was a rise at the end of the war in

1762-3, and a fall once the American war began in 1776. However, it is clear that other factors were also involved: for example, the famine years of 1765-6 also show an increase in vagrancy. Although punishments did tend to be more severe in the 1770s, the magistrates dealt with individuals not with trends. Of the 338 vagrants whose examinations survive in the rolls, 115 were sent to the house of correction, fourteen were ordered to be whipped and the rest, about sixty per cent, were just passed on their way to their place of settlement.

PART II. THE MEANS OF CONTROL

3 TERROR

The first part of this study has tried to show that the 1740s were a time of considerable political and economic instability, and that a wide range of crimes came before the courts. There was a good deal of petty theft; people were prepared to prosecute for trivial assaults; economic regulation generated much business; parish officers presented unmarried mothers and vagrants. There seems to be much truth in the picture of eighteenth-century England as a spontaneous, rumbustious society, a people quick to resort to fists, careful of rights and ardent in resistance to injustice. It was a violent age, brutal in its pleasures and punishments. Many people were so poor that some might be expected to steal to feed their families and others be driven to malevolence by the injustice of extreme class divisions. Without any professional police forces, how was such a society controlled? In particular, how was the crime rate reduced in the middle years of the century? The following chapters try to answer these questions by examining the system of criminal justice in Lindsey at this time.

The traditional answer to the question, 'How was eighteenth-century England controlled?' is well known: by terror. A brutal and barbarous people were held in check by the gallows and the lash. Few criminals could be caught so those convicted suffered extreme punishment, in public, to deter others. There were over 200 capital offences; by the end of the century the death penalty might be inflicted for theft of anything valued at more than one shilling. And public executions were only the pinnacle of the 'bloody penal code'; below was a morass of summary trials, foul prisons, public floggings and the more delicate injustice of arbitrary reprieve.

Some of the Lindsey evidence supports such a picture. Certainly some of the men tried at assizes looked brutal enough: William Sydell, a burglar, was described as 'aged 24, five feet four inches tall, black hair, lost part of his nose'. Charles White, a footpad, had 'a scar on the left cheek and his left leg crooked'. Of his two accomplices, one had 'a scar on his forehead', the other 'his face pitted with smallpox'.[1]

Such men, accused of serious crimes, would be held in the castle at Lincoln. If convicted at assizes they might be returned to the notorious 'pit', a subterranean dungeon for the condemned. Its evils often attracted the attention of the press. In March 1785,

> seven convicts under sentence of death in Lincoln castle attempted to make their escape. A turnkey and two assistants went down into the condemned pit. The convicts seized the man who had the pitchfork to shake up the straw, wrenched the fork from him, and drove them into the pit, fastening them up. The gaoler, Mr Wood, was alarmed, and the convicts were seized and put in double irons.[2]

The pit saw one incident which might well be chosen to exemplify all the worst features of the eighteenth-century system. In 1769 a young man called James Lusby was sentenced to death for sheep stealing. He bought a reprieve by making 'useful discoveries of a most notorious gang of thieves, who have for three years been a terror to the interior part of Lincolnshire'. The authorities arrested two of the gang, but, with astonishing insensitivity, placed them in the same dungeon as poor Lusby. Predictably, 'they entered into a wicked conspiracy' to kill the traitor. This they effected in the evening, 'by knocking him down in the pit, and immediately jumping on his body, by which they broke his ribs and burst his heart'. One of the gang, Matthews, cheerfully confessed to this and to another murder. 'After the judge had passed sentence of death upon him, he desired his lordship would give orders to have him executed early in the morning, that he might dine with the Devil at noon'.[3]

In one sense Matthews was lucky. There were worse punishments than hanging. If a woman murdered her husband she committed petty treason, and was burned at the stake. At Lincoln in 1722

> Eleanor Elsom burnt at the stake for the murder of her husband. She was brought out of the prison barefoot, covered with a tarred cloth, made like a shift, a tarred bonnet on her head, and her legs, feet, and arms also had tar on them. She was put on a hurdle, and drawn on a sledge to the place of execution, near the gallows. After spending some time in prayer the executioner placed her on the tar barrel, about three feet high. A rope, which ran in a pulley through the stake, was fixed about her neck, she herself placing it properly with her hands. The rope being drawn extremely tight with the pulley, the tar-barrel was pushed away, and three irons were fastened round her body to confine it to the stake, that it might not drop when the rope should be burnt. As soon as this was done the fire was kindled, but in all probability she was quite dead before the fire reached her, as the executioner pulled the body several times whilst the irons were being fixed, which took about five minutes. There being a great quantity of tar, and the wood on the pile being quite dry, the fire burnt with amazing fury; notwithstanding which a great part of her could be plainly discerned for nearly half an hour.[4]

No further confirmation of the brutality and horror of the eighteenth-century penal system is needed. But did such measures deter? Were these gruesome exhibitions sufficient to terrify the people into obedience to the law?

Certainly large crowds turned up to watch the executions. In March 1785 over 20,000 people attended the execution of nine felons at Lincoln.[5] Moreover, some of those in authority believed public hangings had a salutary educational value. Henry Best, who grew up in Lincoln in the last years of the century, recalled that his father, a magistrate, encouraged him to attend assizes 'as a school of justice and wisdom'. Best's school reinforced this attitude: 'Our schoolmasters ... dismissed the boys half-an-hour before noon, that they might arrive in time at the place of execution, when there was a man to be hanged'.[6]

Best found the executions horrifying, and liked to tell the story of a senior clergyman from the cathedral. He had a reputation as a tough, awkward character, who suffered fools ill and dissenters not at all. He once took on a whole company of dissenters meeting to petition for the abolition of the slave trade. However, even such a man was shaken when he was unexpectedly required to act as priest at an execution. He 'gave consolation, walked by the side of the condemned man, and stayed to the last. Then, staggering from the excess of his own emotion, he said to the nearest in the crowd, without seeing to whom he spoke, "Lead me away, I beg you, lead me away"'. Best concluded that the effect of public execution 'is the very reverse of edifying, and that it did not deter, for the criminal who has seen one knows he has seen the very worst'.[7]

It might be argued that the 'bloody code' was not quite as bloody in practice as it appeared to be. Certainly the assize calendars of the 1770s suggest some moderation, judged by the standards of the age. Of the eighty-two cases tried at assizes, half ended in acquittal. Six convicts claimed benefit of clergy and were burned in the hand; four were transported. Others were sentenced to short terms of imprisonment, 'sent for a soldier', or bound over to keep the peace. Only thirteen were condemned to death. Of those, earlier press reports lead to a guess that half would have been reprieved. Thus, in ten years only about six people from Lindsey were hanged at Lincoln.

Douglas Hay has argued that the selective use of reprieves was a central feature of the eighteenth-century system of justice and social control.

It allowed the rulers of England to make the courts
a selective instrument of class justice, yet
simultaneously to proclaim the law's incorruptible
impartiality, and absolute determinacy. Their
political and social power was reinforced daily by
the bonds of obligation on one side and
condescension on the other ... . And in the
countryside the power of gentlemen and peers to
punish or forgive worked in the same way to
maintain the fabric of obedience, gratitude, and
deference.[8]

The Lindsey evidence is insufficient to test this assertion,
because the calendars do not tell us if the sentences were carried
out. Other sources give the impression that considerable
numbers were reprieved. The *Annual Register* reported that at
Lincoln Midsummer assizes in 1776 'three were capitally
convicted, but reprieved'; and in July 1778, 'four who received
judgement of death were all reprieved'.[9] Where other sources
mention reprieves they imply they were granted as Blackstone
said they should be, on the recommendation of the judges
'before they left the city'.[10]

Even if the death penalty did not act, or was not used as a
direct deterrent, there is still a sense in which it was central to
the eighteenth-century criminal law. The assize judges who
came to Lincoln were the king's judges, impressive and living
reminders that the justice administered in the most petty case in
the lowest court in the most remote hamlet of the county was
part of a great national system. They appeared and acted as
great men. No less a judge than Blackstone sat at Lincoln.
They ruled on difficult cases which the lower courts had been
unable to determine; they often expounded on recent
developments and national policy. The respect due to them and
to the king's law was seen in the assembly of gentry, many of
them justices and exalted in their own districts but at assizes
doing homage by acting as nothing more than grand jurors.

Indeed the national system of law, the king's peace, was only
a partial revelation. The assizes were intended to impress upon
an illiterate and superstitious people that the king's law was only

a reflection of a higher, universal law, to which all were subject. This mystery was expressed in the elaborate ceremonial of the court, here performed in the perfect setting of the Bail and Close of Lincoln. There was a solemn procession of robed judges, escorted by the high sheriff of the county with his thirty spearmen in blue uniforms and followed by the magistrates, lawyers, and officers of the court. Divine authority was invoked by the assize sermon in the cathedral and the impression sustained by the tolling of Great Tom. The archaic traditions of the court, the famous symbols of the black cap or the white gloves, were all deliberately theatrical customs to express the majesty and authority of the law.[11]

Of course, the people were not fools to be deceived by old men in wigs, but ceremony was more appropriate to their patterns of thought than it is to ours. They made sense of the world in a way which was quite different from the critical, scientific, empirical, literate culture of the twentieth century. The countryman of the eighteenth century used magic, superstition, custom, myth, primitive religion, and close acquaintance with natural phenomena. His world was vivid, organic, 'a polymorphous, animate universe', where each person was part of a greater whole and in which their actions or omissions had consequences, where what they did mattered.[12]

One key element in this 'prior culture', this 'mythical thinking', was the mysterious interconnectedness of all things. This belief had important consequences when a crime was committed: if the natural order had been disturbed by wrongdoing it must be possible to find the culprit. One of the magistrates recorded how he was troubled by an old woman who believed that he must know where her cow might be found, that she lost 't'uther day'.[13]   It was a common practice to use a 'cunning man' to find criminals. Lincoln had a wizard called Wosdel, who performed such services in the early nineteenth century. On one occasion, 'a robbery having been committed at a farm, and no clue being found, ... the farmer's wife persuaded her husband to send for ... Wosdel, who came with his familiar spirit in the form of a blackbird, and soon found out who had committed the robbery and how it was done'. As soon as he arrived at the farm the culprits came into the room and when challenged, immediately accepted Wosdel's discovery. They were both convicted and transported.[14]

The same theme of hidden purpose and order can be found in the Hibaldstow parish register. In 1747 the parish clerk recorded that the 'most fatal distemper amongst the Horned Cattle, ... and that unnatural Rebellion which broke out in Scotland' had been preceded by 'a comet or blazing star which was seen every evening westwardly'. He had no doubt that the disasters which followed this portent were 'the just judgement of Almighty God'.[15]

In all this there was a strong sense of natural law which underpinned the whole system of criminal justice in the popular mind. Blackstone carried the point further. He argued that for offences against natural law, which were evil in themselves, 'capital punishments are in some instances inflicted by the immediate command of God himself' and quoted Biblical and other sources to press the idea. By the standards of the age he was moderate and drew a distinction between 'positive' and 'natural' laws. He warned against the use of the death penalty for mere 'offences of human institution' against 'social rights', but he was clear that it was justified for offences against 'the law of nature'.[16]

In this sense the death penalty was the ultimate expression of the authority of the law. If the law truly represented a universal moral dominion, then it was infinitely greater than any individual and it deserved the power to take a man's life. To remove that power, to suggest the law could not claim such a right, might imply that it was simply a jumble of human expedients. Thus in a traditional society the death penalty played a vital role because it was used to confirm the power and authority of the law. For superstitious people the law was not man-made but was, in a mysterious way, the expression of a higher moral law. Even in remote Lindsey no man might escape its judgement .

4 THE MAGISTRATES

a) Appointment

The 'bloody penal code' is often seen as a fertile environment for the unjust magistrate. Popular fiction during and since the eighteenth century offers many examples of the justice who is a petty tyrant in his district: careful of his woods, his game and his new enclosures, dealing out harsh sentences of imprisonment or flogging after summary conviction in his own parlour. Such men carry the violent oppression of the assizes into the villages and hamlets of rural England to cow the people into submission.

There is little evidence to support this myth of local tyranny in the behaviour of the magistrates in Lindsey between 1740 and 1780. In the first place, there were simply not enough of them to terrorise the county. Lindsey was a remote, backward, rural area, with bleak Wolds, dangerous Fens, and barren wastes. It was far from London, had few towns, and lacked 'good society'. Of course, because land was cheap many gentlemen owned estates there and as many as two hundred wanted to be 'in the Commission', to hold the rank of justice of the peace as a mark of social status. However, few wanted to live in such an area, and many left their estates to agents and stewards; even fewer were prepared to 'take out their Dedimus' and become active justices, forever pestered by the trivial disputes of illiterate country bumpkins.

Throughout the whole of Lindsey in the decade 1740-49 only thirty justices were 'active' and in the two decades 1750-69 the number fell to twenty-five. Moreover, many of these only performed reluctantly, occasionally, if called upon. In any one year between 1740 and 1770 there were only six to ten really active justices who attended sessions regularly and carried the great bulk of the work. These active justices were not evenly distributed: they tended to congregate in 'Spilsbyshire', near Lincoln, around Louth, or (a few) east of Gainsborough. This left some areas, like the northern Wolds, the Marsh and the Ancholme valley around the towns of Caistor, Brigg and Barton, very short of justices indeed. One of the consequences was that it was necessary to appoint more clerical justices than was usual elsewhere. Of the seventy magistrates who were active between 1740 and 1780, fifteen were clergymen. To contemporaries it must have appeared that there were even more, since most of the fifteen were chosen because they were prepared to be vigorous, and to take a great share of the work. Some of them, like the Reverend Henry Best in Lincoln, or the Reverend Justice (his Christian name) Finley at Authorpe, were prominent figures, well known as 'the' local magistrates and regular attenders at quarter sessions.

By this period, to qualify for the bench a gentleman had to own real property worth at least one hundred pounds per annum and be resident in the county to which he was appointed. Magistrates were appointed by the lord chancellor (in the name of the king), on the recommendation of the lord lieutenant of the county. Some of the correspondence of the duke of Ancaster, the lord lieutenant of Lincolnshire, shows the process at work. In 1743 he wrote to lord chancellor Hardwicke:

> My Lord,
>   I acquainted your Lordship some time since that I was desirous that the Commission for the County of Lincoln should be renew'd. I have now for that purpose signed three lists of persons' names which I begg leave to recommend to your Lordship, and I believe such as are proper to be interested.[1]

In fact Ancaster probably had little room for manoeuvre because it was so difficult to find gentlemen willing to act. It seems likely that he decided on his lists after very close consultation with the local magistrates, and frequently he just accepted suggestions from them. Furthermore, we may guess that the magistrates kept an eye open for any new clergyman or estate owner who might make an active JP and ease their burden.

There was a further important consideration and restriction in the appointment of justices. When a new JP took out his Dedimus he had to swear in open court, before one or two of his colleagues, 'that he will be faithful and bear true allegiance to His Majesty King George, ... and renounce, refuse, and abjure any allegiance or obedience to any of the descendants of the late King James II'. A modern study of Kent has shown the substance which lay behind these words.[2] In the late seventeenth and early eighteenth centuries appointments were determined by political allegiance and the need to secure the new dynasty meant purges of Tories and the selection of additional Whigs. Like Kent, other counties have much correspondence on this matter between lord lieutenants and lord chancellors. Unfortunately, the Lincolnshire material is very thin, perhaps because it was so difficult to find enough active magistrates. In 1743 there was some trouble with Mr Fisher, 'a Clergyman in Kesteven, who for some years has been disagreeable to the neighbouring Gentlemen'. Ancaster had him 'mark'd out to be remov'd' in 1742, but he had been saved by the intervention of no less a person than Walpole, the ailing Prime Minister. He wrote to the lord chancellor:

> I have known the Gentleman's character for some time and never heard anything but much to his advantage, and think his Principles and zeal for the government are unquestionable, which I hope will exempt him from being turn'd out, a fate not too frequent among their worships. I have enemies enough, not to make more by being nam'd for concerning myself when I have so little to do.

Ancaster replied that Fisher was so obnoxious that if Hardwicke must nominate him it should be for the neighbouring Parts of Holland.[3]

By the second and third decades of the eighteenth century the fierce divisions of the seventeenth century were moderating and political considerations were playing less of a role in the appointment of magistrates. In 1726 George II had instructed Lord Chancellor King:

> ... to put into the commission of the peace all gentlemen of rank and quality, unless they were in direct opposition to his government, but still to keep a majority of those who were known to be most firmly in his interest.

Thus by 1740 'most commissions were dominated by a Whig majority, but Tory applications ... were no longer always automatically vetoed'.[4] This seems to be a fair description of the situation in Lindsey in the early 1740s. One or two of the old families like the Langtons were JPs, but others, like the Dymokes and the Hickmans, were notably absent from the bench, which was heavily dominated by Whigs.

However, there was a marked change in the late 1740s, especially after 1748. By then three things had happened. The failure of the Tories to rise during the '45 eased the situation. They had admitted that they valued the establishment too much to risk the major upheaval which would be necessary to restore the Stuarts. Their attitude was caught exactly in an incident at a dinner table in one of the Tory strongholds. The great Dr Johnson was a friend of Bennet Langton, son of an ancient Lindsey family, and in 1763 the doctor was dining at the ancestral home at Langton, in the Wolds near Spilsby. Perhaps because 'he was wont to exercise ... his ... ingenuity in talking Jacobitism', perhaps because he wanted to tease his Lincolnshire friends, Johnson shocked the company by taking a young lady by the hand and declaring, 'My dear, I hope you are a Jacobite'. Old Mr Langton, Bennet's father, was mightily offended. He demanded, 'with great warmth', what Johnson meant by putting such a question to his niece. He insisted that although he was 'a high and steady Tory' he was 'attached to the present Royal Family', and he strongly resented the implication of Jacobitism.[5]

That reply might stand for many of the old Lincolnshire

gentry, and it reflected the second change at this time, the more important measures of reconciliation which were taking place at national level. In 1745 the government had declared that, 'In all Commissions of the Peace, hereafter to be issued, all proper Regard shall be had to Gentlemen of Figure and Fortune, well-affected to His Majesty's Government, without distinction of Parties.'[6]

Thirdly, there were administrative changes in the organisation of quarter sessions. Until 1748 each sessions court was adjourned to as many as half-a-dozen little towns in Lindsey. This practice was convenient for the people but it worried the Whigs because the meetings in some towns, for example Gainsborough, might have a majority of Tories on the bench. After 1748 there was only one meeting for the whole of Lindsey each quarter. These meetings were attended by a larger number of magistrates, from the whole of the Parts so any Tories admitted in the new spirit of reconciliation could be kept in a safe minority.

With these local, national and administrative changes old Tory families like the Hickmans and the Massingberds became active, indeed prominent, members of the bench. The end of the old hatreds is neatly caught in an exchange of letters between two old JPs, veterans of the past struggles. In the sessions roll for Michaelmas 1774 there is a note from Sir Nevil Hickman, the Gainsborough Tory, recommending a man for the post of high constable. He sent it for endorsement to the man who had been one of the foremost Whigs in the county for forty years, Thomas Whichcot. As one of the very last things he did as a JP, Whichcot wrote on the letter in a shaky hand, 'I most heartily concur with Sir Nevile Hickman'.[7] Both the sentence and the subject reflect the new air of stability which prevailed from the late 1740s onwards: the old conflicts were dead and the magistrates could concentrate on administrative matters, on running the county.

b) Some Personalities
An examination of the magistrates who bore the brunt of the work reveals three characteristics: a sense of duty to the local community; an active determination to preserve the existing

settlement; and sheer hard work. It was by these means, not by tyranny, that success was achieved.

In 'his country' the best known of the Lindsey magistrates was Thomas Whichcot. Born in 1700 into an old Lincolnshire family, he inherited an estate worth £1,500 per annum and a country house in the small village of Harpswell, conveniently situated about eight miles north of Lincoln and enjoying wide views over the Trent valley. After attending Brigg Grammar School he went up to Cambridge to read classics and mathematics. He seems to have taken his studies seriously and completed his education by entering Gray's Inn, perhaps already thinking of life as a magistrate. He had other opportunities because his family had good connections. There was a rich and eccentric uncle who wanted him to go into business and high finance to restore the family fortunes. The Saundersons, his aristocratic neighbours, were always trying to tempt him to accompany them to London and make a figure in society. Whichcot rejected all such offers, preferring, in his uncle's words, 'to be a Country Gentleman, managing and taking care of his own'.[8]

Partly this was because 'his own' did need taking care of. There were financial difficulties which meant that only the most basic facilities could be maintained at Harpswell. Indeed, economy had driven Whichcot's mother to live in London and she was in favour of selling the place. It was infested with mice, there were no fire grates and guests had to bring their own bedding.[9] Some people thought Whichcot was lazy. His uncle said he was 'unwilling to pursue any difficult study to attain honour or profit' and it is easy to see how he gave that impression.[10] The steward at Harpswell described his lifestyle to his mother:

> He lives very Reservedly at Home, and, I believe, with much more satisfaction than the great ones about St James's. He eats a Piece of Mutton or Beefe very heartily at Noon, and, after dinner, drinks the King's Health and all his friends ... in a Tankard-Toast. Thus Madam my master lives, and is in such a thriving Condition that Jas.

Abraham has been here last Week to let out his Clothes.[11]

Namier and Brooke make the point that, although he was an MP for thirty years, he very rarely spoke in the House.

There was more to it than indolence. He does appear to have been a man of some principle. Towards the end of his life he described himself as 'one of the last of the old Whigg-race, now almost extinct', who believed in 'all those blessings which our laws and religion obtained by the Revolution' which had rescued the country from 'that bigoted and arbitrary Prince, of odious memory, James II'.[12] He was one of those independent Whig country gentlemen who believed it was necessary to be working constantly to preserve and consolidate the Hanoverian settlement. He was a county MP for Lincolnshire for over thirty years, from 1740 until 'age and infirmity' forced him to retire in 1774. He may not have spoken much in the Commons but he campaigned vigorously against the Tories in the 1720s, subscribed £500 against the Pretender in 1745 and did speak and campaign to support the wool interest in the 1770s.

However, it was local activity he really believed in. A gentleman must play his part in running the county. He resisted the temptations of London and foreign travel offered by his wealthy friends and, as his steward reported,

Enjoys a Perfect state of Health and stays much at home, unless when Publick business calls him away. He has been four or five times upon the Commission of Sewers, and is to meet the Commissioners again next Wednesday. He takes a deal of Pains to Understand the method of Proceeding, and will, (I dare say) soon be a master of it.[13]

He took most pains over his work as a JP. He was by far the most active magistrate in Lindsey and was known locally as 'Justice Whichcot'. From 1740 until 1768 he rarely missed a quarter sessions, attending not only the local meetings in his own division, but also travelling to Louth and Spilsby. Once, when he was called to attend a meeting about the enclosure of the Fens arranged for sessions week, he wrote to the clerk of the peace asking him to postpone the sessions which, he said, 'I would not miss on any account'.[14]

As far as it is possible to tell he seems to have been a fair and kindly magistrate. At Christmas he kept open house at Harpswell for a week, offering local people beef and beer. He even had something of a reputation as a protector of the rights of the poor, as Sir Charles Anderson recalled:

> I recollect my father telling me that when Sir Cecil Wray made his park at Fillingham and enclosed it with a wall, he obstructed a right of way across from the villages of Harpswell, Hemswell, and Glentworth to the great Lincoln road. Mr Whichcot once a year used to order his coach and four, and, attended by a lot of labourers, used to drive up to the park wall (built up of loose stone with a building course on top), pull it down, drive through the breach across the park to the opposite side next the Lincoln road, where the same was done. He then drove back. Sir Cecil then built it up, and the next year old Whichcot did the same, up to the time of his death, when no-one else was patriotic enough to keep up the right, which of course fell into disuetude. [15]

Another regular attender at quarter sessions with a good reputation was George Stovin (1696-1780) of Crowle in the Isle of Axholme. Like Whichcot, he came from an old Lincolnshire family. The legend was that the strung bow of their crest signified that an ancestor had been chief bow-stringer in the Conqueror's army. The Stovins were also of the Whig tradition and had good reason to believe in religious toleration: a former George Stovin had been imprisoned in Lincoln castle for his Quakerism and had died there. Again like Whichcot, Stovin preferred life in his own country, although perhaps he was not so well educated:

> He was not brought up to any profession, but led
> the life of a country gentleman ... taking great
> interest in the affairs of the neighbourhood. He
> scarcely ever left the Levels, living at Crowle ...,
> thinking no part of England comparable to
> Axholme, no town equal to Crowle. [16]

When he married in 1726 he built a small house in Crowle
which he called 'Justice Hall' and dedicated himself to the work
of being a local magistrate. He was very active and rarely
missed a sessions. A famous story is told of him. When John
Wesley was preaching at Epworth in 1737 some of the enraged
inhabitants put the Methodists in a cart and carried them to
Stovin's house. He asked the mob, 'What was their complaint?'
At first there was an awkward silence, until

> one old man said, 'An't please your worship, they
> have converted my wife. Till she went among
> them she had such a tongue, and now she is quiet
> as a lamb.' 'Carry them back, carry them back',
> said Stovin, 'and let them convert all the scolds in
> the town'.[17]

His 'quiet and sober life' was marred by tragedies. Five of
his children died, including his oldest son George, who was,
perhaps, also being prepared for the duties of magistrate as he
had been entered at Gray's Inn. The death of his wife in 1745
seems to have affected him greatly, and probably contributed to
his decision to give up his work on the bench in 1749. Much of
his energy was now spent on his favourite antiquarian
researches. He moved from his beloved Crowle to Winterton,
from where there is an attractive picture of him on old age, 'by
one that knew him well',

> living ... in a little cottage which he had made
> arcadian with honeysuckle and other flowers, where
> he was to be seen every morning at five with his
> pipe. Having a good memory, and full of anecdote,
> he was accustomed to amuse his neighbours. [18]

Whichcot and Stovin reflected many of the characteristics of the other magistrates. Several, like Whichcot, were also members of parliament. They included Henry Pacey, John Harrison, Robert Vyner, Coningsby Sibthorp, and Sir Cecil Wray. Others were men of energy and ability. Charles Chaplin of Tathwell was a well-known agricultural improver, of sufficient standing to challenge Bakewell to a sheep-breeding contest. Sir Cecil Wray's agricultural experiments were famous and he was one of the very few Lindsey gentlemen praised by Arthur Young during his first tour of the county in 1771. Some had reputations for liberal or progressive views. Wray wanted reconciliation with America and was a member of the Yorkshire Association for Parliamentary Reform. In 1782 he was elected MP for the popular constituency of Westminster along with the celebrated Charles James Fox. His proposer was another Lindsey JP, Lawrence Monck of Caenby. John Harrison, MP for Grimsby and an active justice, was also a supporter of Fox.[19] Robert Vyner was 'one of the most prolific speakers of his time, (who) acted consistently against every Administration'. Lord Egmont wrote that he was 'a whimsical man, full of projects of reformation, especially about the army and the militia'. Perhaps it was these interests that led him to 'swear like a dragoon'.[20]

There are several minor pieces of evidence which might be interpreted as revealing tolerance, or at least some concern for the poor, by several of the magistrates. Chaplin provided small plots of land so that labourers might keep one or two cows.[21] Thomas Goulton, although he condemned the labourers' wives as 'doing nothing but bring children and eat cake', thought most labouring men 'sober and industrious'.[22] At Christmas 1740 one of the clerical magistrates, the Revd. John Russell, wrote to the clerk of the peace about a case pending at sessions. A neatherd was prosecuting a farmer for refusal to pay wages. Russell urged that the farmer be charged the maximum possible fees, 'for the poor neatherd ought to have been paid his wages without trouble'.[23]

The bulk of the work seems to have been done by men like Stovin: solid local gentry who simply felt that the area had to be governed, and took the multitude of petty duties upon themselves. The people called them 'Justice' or 'Squire' and the best examples of these workhorses were Robert Cracroft of Hackthorn; David Atkinson of Fanthorpe; William Marshall of Theddlethorpe; John Uppleby of Wootton; Henry Best of Lincoln; the aptly-named Justice Finley of Authorpe; Bentley Bennet of Utterby; William Allenby of North Thoresby; Robert Morton; and Lawrence Monck of Caenby.

One of the constant themes of these men is the importance of their own locality, their own county and suspicion or dislike of the central government. Whichcot and Stovin's preferences were clear from the life they chose. Vyner 'insisted he was for nothing but his country .... The principles on which we tender our services, setting aside the cant words of the country interest, are independency and uncorruption.'[24] It was an attitude which united Whigs and Tories. Old Bennet Langton, writing to Joseph Banks during that cold winter of 1739-40, described the state of the country as

> warr and taxes at four shillings in the pound ... As the case is at present the merchants and moneyed people by their smuggling and illicit trade have been chiefly instrumental in bringing on the warr, and the country gentlemen must be at the expense of it without their contributing one farthing towards it.

And, his fellows might have added, the same country gentlemen were left with the unpaid everyday work of governing the county.

c) Summary Justice

In their *Village Labourer*, the Hammonds warned of the dangers of 'single justices out of sessions':

> Magistrates could administer in this uncontrolled capacity a drastic code for the punishment of vagrants and poachers without jury or publicity. The single justice himself determined all questions of law and of fact, and could please himself as to the evidence he chose to hear. In 1822 the duke of

Buckingham tried and convicted a man of coursing on his estate. The trial took place in the duke's kitchen: the witnesses were the duke's keepers.[26]

Did such injustice take place in Lindsey between 1740 and 1780? Unfortunately there are no good records of individual magistrates at work during those years. The earliest evidence we have are the 'Justice Books' of Thomas Dixon of Riby, for the years 1788 to 1798.[27] By that time the atmosphere had changed, harshened by the French Revolution, the long wars and deteriorating living conditions for the poor. Even so, if these changes are borne in mind Dixon's books are valuable indicators of the role of summary justice in the eighteenth century. He was very careful to ape existing practice.

Thomas Dixon (1728-98) came from a family of tenant farmers who had prospered and bought land in the second half of the eighteenth century. From 1758 until his death in 1798 he farmed at Riby, a small village in the north of the county, just where the Marsh met the Wolds. He was an important and active figure in the locality, but still a wealthy farmer rather than ancient gentry. He served as churchwarden, overseer, and surveyor of the highways for Riby at various times between 1759 and 1787. His increasing economic and social status was crowned when he became a magistrate in 1787 at the age of fifty-nine.

Perhaps it was the novelty of the bench, the inexperience of his line of the family in such matters, a concern to make sure he got things right, which made him the only magistrate to leave records. He had no legal training and no close neighbour to guide him. These were not insurmountable problems. For many years isolated rural magistrates had been guided by reference manuals like Dalton's *Countrey Justice*, which explained the law and legal procedures, defined the JP's duties, and offered advice. Mr Dixon seems to have used *The Justice of the Peace and Parish Officer*, by Richard Burn. The four leather-backed volumes of Burn's *Justice* were to become the most popular of all such guides. Its many pages of close print gave detailed and clear expositions of the most complex matters and the busy magistrate was aided by marginal notes and subject headings, in alphabetical order, at the top of each page.

The other important aid for a rural justice was a clerk. The most active JPs used members of their estate or household staff; sometimes the local high constable was employed. Mr Dixon seems to have liked to keep his own records, although he certainly used an assistant for some things. He was fastidious. The notebooks are small and informal, but there is no sense of the careless squire dispensing rough justice in his own territory. Rather the impression is of a man new to a job, surrounded by knowledgeable clients and superiors, anxious to do a complex task exactly according to the rules. He noted the times and dates of quarter sessions and laboriously copied out the forms of certain warrants and documents that a magistrate used regularly. These were taken from Burn unnecessarily, because there was a well-known printer in Lincoln called John Rose, 'opposite the Angel Inn, above hill, where may be had all sorts of Warrants, etc.'.[28]

One of the incidents recorded in the notebooks is a good example of how summary justice worked. It was, of course, entirely a system of private prosecutions, so Dixon waited until someone came to his house at Riby with an 'information and complaint'. Over three-quarters of the complainants were farmers or parish officers. Many of the complaints were heard on Mondays, perhaps because Dixon tried to ease the demands on his time by being available for routine, non-urgent business on that day. This case was not heard on a Monday.

On Friday, 22 January 1796, William Russell knocked on Dixon's door. He had walked or ridden about three miles from Brocklesby, along a road which overlooked the Marsh, and which still catches the north-east wind that blows on to this coast in January. We may imagine he approached confidently, and he may even have been wearing a livery of some sort, for he was 'Gamekeeper to the Right Honourable Charles, Lord Yarborough', of Brocklesby Hall. Admitted to Dixon's presence, he declared that in the village of Great Limber on the Yarborough estate there 'hath resided ... for one year last past and upwards', a labourer 'whose real name is not known, but who is commonly called or known as Yorkshire Tom'. This intriguing character apparently kept two greyhounds, and on the previous Sunday, 17 January, he had used them 'in the Park of

Great Limber', to 'kill one hare'. What had happened during the week to discover this is not recorded. Perhaps the coursing had been witnessed, perhaps the hare had been found in the possession of the accused, perhaps the common knowledge of the labourers had been betrayed by careless gossip. At any rate Russell satisfied Dixon, not only that there was a case to answer, but that he had witnesses to support him. Dixon therefore issued a warrant 'to arrest Yorkshire Tom' and bring him 'to my house at Riby on Wednesday 27 January at twelve noon'. Russell took the warrant and gave it to the constable of Limber to execute.

Accordingly, next Wednesday, Russell, Yorkshire Tom, the constable, and at least one witness, turned up at Riby. There Dixon 'duly examined the proofs and allegations' and decided that Tom was guilty. There was a standard penalty for a first offence and he was 'convicted in the sum of five pounds'. As often happened in such cases Tom was unable to pay and, as 'it appears on the oath of the ... Constable that the said Yorkshire Tom is not a housekeeper nor possessed of any visible property', he was sentenced to three months' imprisonment in the new house of correction at Kirton Lindsey. Dixon issued the necessary documents for the constable and the keeper of the house of correction. Armed with these and hiring either two horses or a waggon, the constable set off with the prisoner on the fifteen-mile winter journey across the Wolds to Kirton. When he was released in April Tom would have to make his own way home.[29]

This case reflects the popular image of summary justice in the eighteenth century: poaching, squire dispensing justice in his own parlour and severe penalties. However, such cases seem to have been far fewer than we might expect. In the ten years 1788 to 1798 Mr Dixon summarily convicted just thirteen people, about one each year. Tom was the only poacher. The most severe penalties were inflicted on troublesome servants like Thomas Ashby of Healing, who was convicted for 'swearing at his master ... and giving his Victuals to the dogs'; or Rebecca Green of Irby, who was 'hired for a year last May Day as a servant in husbandry', and had since been 'guilty of several misdemeanour and particularly neglecting her work and refusing to obey the reasonable commands of her master and has absented herself from her master's service'. In the ten-year period Dixon convicted six such servants and in five of the cases imposed the standard penalty of three months in the house of correction. The other one was imprisoned for one month.[30]

Two of the other convictions were for damage and trespass: Hannah Wells was ordered to pay ten shillings for 'satisfaction and charges' for 'tearing and breaking down hedges in Laceby'; Christopher Hobbins was dealt with more harshly when he 'cut up several young oaks growing in a certain wood in Roxton'. He was fined forty shillings with six shillings costs and being unable to pay was sent to the house of correction 'for one month and to be whipped privately within the last week of the said month'.[31]

The remaining summary convictions were comparatively trivial. Robert Rollinson of Rothwell, blacksmith, was convicted 'for profane cursing and swearing' and was fined at the standard rate of one shilling for each oath, two shillings in all. Three men were convicted of 'being drunk on Sunday' and 'paid the penalty of five shillings according to the direction of the Statute in such cases made, being the first offence'.[32]

Summary convictions were not the whole of Mr Dixon's work. Recorded in another place in his Justice Books were sixty 'informations and complaints' which he heard in the ten-year period. Forty of these were 'master and servant' disputes. No verdicts were recorded for these cases. No doubt some were referred to the higher court of petty sessions. Others would have been settled by informal agreement or allowed to lapse when tempers had cooled. Thomas Ashby, quoted above as sentenced to three months after swearing at his employer, was in fact released on the day he was committed because his master went to Dixon 'and pray'd his release and discharge'.[33]

It is not possible to say if the account given by Mr Dixon's books is typical of the out-of-sessions work of Lindsey magistrates in the eighteenth century. The only evidence of such work by the other magistrates is in the sessions rolls. It was customary for JPs to enrol their summary convictions at sessions, but there was great variation in practice: some magistrates were more conscientious than others; some statutes required such enrolment (for example, profane oaths), while others (most notably poaching), did not. Some enrolments may have been lost. None of Mr Dixon's thirteen summary convictions are in the rolls.

There are just eighty-two summary convictions in the sessions rolls for the whole of Lindsey between 1740 and 1780. About sixty of these seem to have been for minor assaults. Until 1747 such cases had usually been dealt with by binding over to keep the peace, but then a new procedure appears to have become popular: the conviction for profane oaths. There were forty-six summary convictions for this offence and it seems that the magistrates were using it as a device. Two quarrelling parties would appear, claim assault and demand justice. The JP would arbitrate and end the trivial dispute by imposing a fine for swearing on the more blameworthy party. Presumably there were very few such squabbles which had not involved at least one oath. This satisfied the complainant, repaired the breach of the king's peace and satisfied the offender with an immediate fixed penalty rather than the more cumbersome binding over. The penalty was decreed at one shilling per oath and thus punishment could be nicely tuned to fit the case. The usual number was one; there were several of two to five, a few of twenty; and the record was held by Christopher Peacock, convicted of forty in 1762.[34]

Of the other summary convictions eight were for selling ale without a licence, carrying the penalty of forty shillings for a first offence. Only four summary convictions for poaching were enroled: two of those so convicted were fined five pounds, one one pound, and one was sent to the house of correction for three months. Four people were convicted of breaking hedges and cutting underwood: three of them were fined sums of up to one pound; the other was sent to the house of correction in Louth, from which he escaped. The remaining convictions were for a variety of minor matters, which both prosecutors and accused probably agreed to have dealt with summarily, as in the case of Sarah Brown who embezzled some hemp 'which she took to spin' from a Nottingham factor.[35]

In short, the recorded number of summary convictions is surprisingly low. Obviously some of the convictions were not enrolled, but even allowing for this the impression from Mr

Dixon's books and the sessions rolls is clear: summary justice was not much used.

d) Opposition

There is a famous old Lincolnshire story about the Barrow-upon-Humber JP, George Uppleby. One dark night in 1816 he was travelling to London in the Lincoln coach when it was stopped near Grantham by two highwaymen. One of them put a pistol to Uppleby's head when, according to the legend, the other exclaimed, 'Why, that's Squire Uppleby, you mayn't shoot our Squire Uppleby.'[36]

If the reality was not quite as cosy as that, it is still difficult to find evidence of hostility or opposition to the magistrates among the people they governed. There are some hints that James Bateman of Well may have been unpopular. In 1748 Richard Willows, a blacksmith, was accused of 'abusing James Bateman Esq. in the execution of his office'. Apparently he was before Bateman on a charge of assaulting two women.[37] There was a more serious case in September 1750. Three butchers, a plumber and a woman, all from Alford, were accused of 'threatening' Bateman. The threats must have been considerable, because the five accused were bound in £1000, £500, £200, and £150 to keep the peace. These were by far the highest sureties demanded of ordinary people in the period 1740 to 1780.[38]

There are two other minor examples of hostility to JPs in the later 1740s. In 1746, during a drunken riot in the Bail of Lincoln, which involved some soldiers, the constables, and the customers and keepers of a bawdy house, a labourer called Samuel Royston was arrested 'for offering sixpence to any person that would tell the Justice he was a fool'.[39] In 1748 there is a brief note that a wheelwright 'challenged and abused' George Stovin.[40] After 1750 even this low level of abuse decreases. There were only two cases of verbal or physical attacks on justices between 1750 and 1780, both committed by the same man, the troublesome George Atterby of Theddlethorpe, a grazier. In 1766, 'on Wednesday last at Louth he did stand and abuse William Marshall Esq., JP, in the execution of his office, and in open court did slander and abuse the said William Marshall'.[41] For this he was committed to the house of correction until he could find sureties of £40 and £20. Ten years later he was up before the Reverend Gideon Bouyer, JP, 'who made such order as he thought reasonable, whereupon George Atterby assaulted the said Revd Mr Bouyer, and did openly declare with several profane oaths and imprecations that he had not done justice to him'. No doubt the scene loses something in the formal words of the charge, but when the case came to trial at sessions the jury took Atterby's part and he was acquitted.[42]

So, in all, there are only six recorded cases of attacks on justices between 1740 and 1780, most of them verbal and of a trivial nature. Perhaps the fact that four of them took place in the late forties has some significance, but considering that two were against one magistrate and two were perpetrated by one 'character', it is impossible to interpret this evidence as revealing any general hostility towards the bench.

There was one major outburst of protest against the magistrates and it offers a glimpse of attitudes 'from below', albeit in exceptional circumstances. In June 1757 the government passed the new Militia Act which required each parish to provide a man to serve in the militia for up to three years. The man was to be chosen by ballot and was to be unpaid. The measure provoked immediate and widespread rioting, not only in Lincolnshire but throughout the country. In Lindsey, James Bateman of Well was again the object of attack. He and Samuel Dashwood received an anonymous letter which referred to the magistrates as 'Buntin Ars'd Coated fellows ... the Just-Asses and Other start-up Officers that buy a Commission for a Trifle and Sells his Nation to make his fortune'.[43] The authors threatened that if the Act was put into operation, they will raise an Army

> ... and beat, Pull down and destroy, all the Gentlemen's Seats in this County ... for they Swear they will not fight for your Estates, they will fight for their own lives first and so begin at home ... and they swear if this go forward they'll have a fair knock at most of your Houses in a small time too.

Justice Lawrence Monck at Caenby seems to have been a particular target. Monck was a wealthy London merchant who had married into an ancient Lincolnshire family, and had been an active magistrate only since 1749. The rioters said they attacked him because 'it was Reported Amongst them that Mr Monck was Busy in the Militia Act' and that 'he had said if the People wou'd not enter into it he wou'd force them, that they shou'd be handcuff'd. That Poor men were good for nothing but to be shot at, and some few more Expressions tending to show Illwill towards Poor Men.'

It was rumoured that a mob 'determined to go to Mr Monck's in a Riotous Manner ... and to Pull down his House'. Monck, 'knowing well the disposition and Manners of the Country People, and his house being Two Miles from his Town, and no nearer than the Distance of one mile to any house', was 'a little Alarm'd and apprehended some Danger'. However, having 'Packt up his Small Papers of Value and carried them to Lincoln' for safety, he returned home and used one of his tenants as an intermediary to arrange a meeting with the rioters. This was successful, 'and in the afternoon about forty persons went to Mr Monck'. They absolutely refused to accept the Militia Act and were 'determin'd not to conform to it', but Monck was able to convince them that he had not said the words imputed to him and that he was not hostile to the poor. The rioters 'drank plentifully, ask'd for some Money to make them drink at home, Received Two Guineas and departed Cheerfully'.

However, the next day Monck was out riding when 'at about Two Miles distance from his House' he 'Accidentally met a mob of Farmers, Labourers, and Country Servants' from other villages. At first 'he did not know one person amongst them', but 'They look'd very surly and ... said they were going to Mr Monck's house.' Monck tried to address them, 'and desired they wou'd be silent, which they consented to, saying, hear him! hear him! lets hear Reason!' He explained that the Ill Reports which they had heard of him were false and that he had 'Satisfied Two Towns, which he understood were to have met them in Their Expedition'. At this the mob 'chang'd their countenances and began to say they wou'd do him no hurt, but many of them at the same time Swore they would knock every Country Gentleman on the Head, for that they wou'd not be dragg'd away from their families, and sent abroad'. To this Monck replied 'that the Act of Parliament had provided that they shou'd not be sent abroad'. When the protesters said that parliament had deceived them, Monck retorted, 'That an Act of Parliament never had deceived them, nor was likely ever to do so'. Significantly, the mob agreed 'That if Parliament was not to be trusted there would be an end of all things'. Monck's day ended as before:

> He went home, and they follow'd him; He gave them Victuals and Drink, yet some of them struck sev'ral Times at the Window Shutters with their Clubs, but were Push'd off by some farmers; Others strove to get into the House at the doors, but were repuls'd in like Manner; Others ask'd for Some money to drink, and being ask'd how much They wou'd have, They said a Guinea a Town. They call'd out their Constables to take the Money for them, and Received Six Guineas for Six Towns.

The area was restless and the people were threatening for several days afterwards. Monck sent them 'a Guinea to be spent amongst them on condition that they wou'd be Quiet', but other villages continued to be 'in Motion', so 'reflecting that the Pacifying such people depended more upon Humour than Reason, and his family being already Teriffy'd, He immediately Took his family to Lincoln'.

These events can be interpreted in a variety of ways as evidence of the relationship between the magistrates and the people. On the one hand it is clear that Bateman and Monck were not popular: the people believed that Monck could have said the words attributed to him and that he did 'shew Ill will towards Poor Men'. There was some resentment of the wealth of the gentry and 'their long green purses'. A growing distance between the gentry and the poor is revealed in the physical isolation of Monck's house and the gulf between his 'Reason' and the mere 'Humour' of the mob.

On the other hand, the circumstances were very exceptional. Indeed it is difficult to imagine conditions more nicely calculated to create hostility to the magistracy. The harvest of 1756 had been poor and the price of wheat had risen from forty-six shillings in January 1757 to sixty shillings in July. In a letter to Dashwood and Bateman there is mention of 'the rott last year'. The Militia Act was so insensitive it might have been deliberately contrived to stir the people against the magistrates: it threatened to take men ignorant of the outside world away from their homes and families and it offered no payment. Above all, it seemed deliberate sharp practice in favour of the rich against the poor because the parish ballot replaced the previous system by which the gentry had been required to provide or pay for an infantry man. The rioters made this point in their letter: 'for they think it more for want of money than men, and they say if you wou'd have men rais'd you may raise them by the Assistance of your long green purses, and be dam'd if you will'. Finally, the Act made sure everyone knew about the measure and offered the perfect occasion for rioting by requiring constables to go round their parishes making lists of those likely to be balloted.

Even in these conditions the strength of the established order is impressive. Monck, who was not one of the old popular JPs by any means, indeed, a new man, an 'incomer', 'busy in the Militia Act', was able to approach, speak to and pacify the rioters. The farmers acted as intermediaries to establish dialogue between him and the protesters. There was apparently respect for parliament and the necessity for good government, taken to almost comic lengths when the mob demanded money to drink and 'call'd out their Constables to take the Money for them', at the precise rate of 'a Guinea a Town'. The disturbances were conducted almost as a ritual negotiation, by known paths and within a deep and established structure. There was never any threat of chaos or revolution, even though some of the gentry had a fright. On 19 September Ancaster reported to London, 'The County is at present tolerably quiet, but from these disturbances each individual may be doubtful how long his property may be his own.'[44] He exaggerated, and after the revised Militia Act of 1758, as David Neave concludes:

'When less than two years later during a period when a French invasion was feared, the North and South Lincolnshire Regiments of Militia were formed, there is no record of any unrest'.[45]

This searchlight into the views of the people is best read as a singular, exceptional crisis and many aspects of it confirm what other evidence suggests: there was very little hostility towards the magistrates; their authority and justice was accepted; the system of local government and justice was very strong. Perhaps the most decisive argument comes from the analysis of the criminal records of quarter sessions where such a high proportion of the complaints and indictments were brought by ordinary people. They trusted the magistrates to do justice to them and had confidence in the system.

5 THE COURT OF QUARTER SESSIONS

Four times each year, at Epiphany (January), Easter (April), Midsummer (July), and Michaelmas (October), the active magistrates met in quarter sessions. In Lindsey it needs only a little imagination to see these eighteenth-century courts. The old buildings still stand at Spital in the Street, the courthouse bearing an inscription which has been translated as:

> This court does right,
> Loves Peace,
> Preserves the Laws,
> Rewards the righteous cause.[1]

In several of the sessions towns the market squares retain the pattern of two centuries ago. Spilsby is a good example. The plain eighteenth-century town hall where sessions were held still stands in the middle of the rectangular market place. Just across the square from it is the imposing White Hart inn to which the magistrates adjourned in the afternoon to deal with administrative business. Between the two was a convenient space where some of the floggings took place at the rising of the court.

The importance and success of the sessions were reflected by the enormous numbers of people who attended. Even in this thinly-populated area where each sessions might be adjourned to as many as six little towns each meeting required a huge, bustling, concourse of people. They crowded the inns and packed the market squares, urgent for the ten o'clock start. There were magistrates and their clerks arriving in coaches, perhaps with some servants; also in a coach was the clerk of the peace with his deputies, books, and papers; there were attorneys and their assistants; high constables (usually two from each wapentake); petty constables (one from each parish); local officials like treasurers and surveyors of the highways; sheriff's bailiffs, anxiously checking to see if all the jurors they had summoned had turned up; and the jurors themselves, at least sixteen for the grand jury, and a dozen or so for a petty jury. Then there were the prosecutors, determined to solve the often long-running feuds which had eventually driven them to law, marshalling their witnesses; and finally there were the accused, the lucky ones travelling from their homes to answer to their bonds. The less fortunate were brought from the house of correction by cart or on foot, but often in chains, led by the keeper of the house. In his cart he also carried some of the weightier legal tomes needed at sessions and a selection of his cats o'nine tails, for it was one of his duties to flog offenders at the end of the proceedings. In all, anything over one hundred people must have attended. Sessions day was a grand and turbulent occasion in the lives of these towns and their surrounding districts.

All this hustle and bustle, the spontaneity and colour of early morning on sessions day in Spilsby, tended to confirm some magistrates' view of the chaotic state of the lower orders. It was not a reasonable system of government in the modern sense. Modern systems expect major and unceasing changes to be the order of things; the emphasis is on individual rights, especially people's right 'to get on with their own lives'; government is active at many levels and is supported by a vast professional bureaucracy. If a problem occurs it is expected that the professional politicians and their officials will develop a new policy to deal with it.

The eighteenth-century system was very different, but it was coherent and effective. The central idea which held the whole system together was the notion of the king's peace, a constant, unchanging and perfect order, which it was the duty of every citizen to uphold. If an assault took place the king's peace had been broken and it was the duty of the victim to bring proceedings; if a road was out of repair it was the duty of the parish to restore the king's highway to the standard required by his majesty. Without a busy bureaucracy offenders were not vigorously pursued, but once a breach of the king's peace had been recorded the system was relentless and implacable in keeping the culprit bound to appear before the king's justices and make restitution. That standard, the king's peace, must be upheld. It was a conception which made for active citizenship. The emphasis was on duty: duty to serve unpaid; duty to prosecute; duty to keep the king's peace in everyday conduct. It also made for stability: peace, property, and individual rights could only be preserved within the king's peace and therefore it was in the interest of all to be active in maintaining that perfect standard.

The central idea of the king's peace was not the only thing which quickened the old system. Another vital factor was that all the business of the sessions was initiated by the people. There was no police force or other official body to bring charges. If your goose was stolen it was up to you to find the thief, gather witnesses and bring the prosecution. A sessions case might require time away from work, a tedious journey, and substantial costs. Moreover, it must have been a daunting prospect for a prosecutor to plunge into the melee of quarter sessions with his bonds and witnesses, trying to understand the rapid procedures. One of the magistrates scribbled the following instructions for a timid servant who had to bring an action. On arrival at sessions he was to

> Enquire for Mr Chapman, Clerk of the Peace, at the White Hart in Gainsborough, and tell him you are come to indict Susannah Poulton (now in the House of Correction for stealing two horseshoes). There is one Corbridge, another felon in the House of Correction who will be indicted.[2]

Yet the people did prosecute, for the law was an integral and essential part of everyday life. Without the law many vital aspects of life could not go on, and the people would have no protection. When cattle trampled the open-field crops, when someone overstocked the common, when the master abused his servant, when a husband beat his wife, when a fight broke out in a pub., and for a host of petty but essential things, the people went to law. The English were a litigious lot.

After the idea of the king's peace and the active participation of the people, the third key element at quarter sessions was the work of the dozens of citizens who did duty as parish officers. They were not professional bureaucrats; they performed part-time and unpaid and they found many of their tasks burdensome, so they did not go looking for work. Nevertheless, they conscientiously performed the services necessary to keep the parish going and they brought much business to sessions. They included: overseers of the poor concerned with poor law disputes, settlement cases and bastardy bonds; surveyors of the highways arguing about boon works, highway rates and what was or was not an adequate state of roads; churchwardens worried about the condition of their churchyard and sometimes presenting general problems of their villages; constables with their warrants and rates and records and presentments of the condition of their parishes; high constables with their lists of expenses for their wapentakes, 'freeholders' bills' of those liable to serve on juries and their numerous presentments of unlicensed ale houses. All these reflected a vigorous system of community self-government, and these 'middling orders' in rural England, these active citizens, were another vital ingredient in making the system of justice work.

a) The Opening of the Court

One of the key figures in the system was the clerk of the peace. Indeed, especially in the first half of the eighteenth century when the sessions were adjourned from place to place, there was a sense in which the clerk of the peace was the quarter sessions in the popular eye because it was only when he and his coach, his books, his papers, and his assistants came to town, bearing the king's commission that the business might begin.

There was a single clerk for the whole of Lindsey, appointed by the duke of Ancaster (as *custos rotulorum*), on the advice of the magistrates. He had to be a man of substance, 'learned in the law'. From 1720 until 1749 the position was held by Henry Sapsford. The clerk was at the hub of everything at sessions: all correspondence, bonds, and documents were sent to him; he orchestrated the proceedings; he was responsible for framing the indictments, advising the justices on points of law, and keeping all records and documents. New clerks of the peace seem to have made major changes in the administration of sessions.

There were also important lesser officials: the clerk of the peace appointed deputies who, no doubt, did much of the routine work. Lindsey was divided into sessional divisions, and each had its own clerk and treasurer. Of the latter, Mr Chipsey Hornsby of Caistor seems to have been prominent. Unfortunately, not much can be recovered about these men. They produced all the records yet, like good officials, they remain shadowy figures. There is no discussion of their role in the evidence, but perhaps it is significant that no major complaints were registered against them in the forty years 1740 to 1780.

Once the clerk had made the arrangements for the sessions - one bill includes 'hire of hall' and 'candles' - the magistrates could take their places. In the 1740s when sessions were adjourned from place to place, attendances at each sitting could be very small, commonly only two or three. As a general rule magistrates only attended sessions in their own local division and each division had its own chairman. A few justices, like Whichcot, attended other sessions as well, perhaps because they were exceptionally conscientious, perhaps because there was a particular piece of business they wished to deal with, or perhaps because the clerk had suggested that the bench might be short of a qualified, experienced magistrate at the next meeting. Such devotion to duty had some financial reward. Magistrates were paid four shillings a day for their attendance at sessions, and the minutes always begin with the clerk's marginal note, 'I paid these Justices'.

If an active magistrate was unable to attend sessions he would send his bonds, documents and convictions to the clerk of the peace, either in advance, or by the hand of his own clerk on the first day of sessions. Justice Harrison's clerk sent a packet of such documents to the clerk at Easter 1742, with the following note:

Hon'd Sir,

   I have sent you half-a-doz. recognizances, to wit, four for Spittle and two for Caistor. My master gives his service to you but is now at Scarborough, and I am, Sir,
your humble Servant,
   John Belton.
I sent these by a friend from Brigg with the examinations inclosed, hoping you get them betimes in the morning. J.Belton.
There is recognizances on both sides of the little paper.[3]

Frequently the JP endorsed one of the recognizances, or enclosed a note in his package of documents, further explaining the circumstances of the case and recommending an appropriate punishment. When the death of his wife forced the conscientious George Stovin to miss a sessions, he wrote:

Worthy Sir,

   I have sent a recog. taken of one Jno. Gaythorn for refusing to pay wages to Mary Johnson - he lives in this parish lately comed from Yorkshire Eastoft where he had wearied all the Justices in the West Riding for seven years last past.

   I have also sent you the examination of Ellen Warren who swears she is the wife of Thos. Warren. The man was apprehended after her and swears his name is Thos. Burroughs, so that one of them is forsworn. There is also a pass which is counterfeit, wherein you will see that the woman went by the name of Jane Burroughs, a soldier's widow. The man beg'd in Crowle for loss of cattle, and they are two old offenders and I think ought to be made examples of.

   I must begg you would excuse my Clerk Mr Crabe's attendance at this Sessions, I having occasion for his keep upon the melancholy occasion of my dear companion's death, and am

here amongst the Crys and Tears of my Dear
children.
> Your sorely distress'd and afflicted servt.,
> Geo Stovin.

One Wm Robinson proves the vagrancy of the man
at Crowle.[4]

Such a letter no doubt reflects what Mr Stovin would have
told his fellow magistrates if he had been on the bench as usual.

Many of the magistrates who did attend the sessions faced
long and difficult journeys of perhaps ten or fifteen miles, a
serious and uncomfortable business in winter. Their irritation
and discomfort showed. Often the first document in the rolls is
a justice's presentment 'on my own view' of the intolerable state
of the roads they had travelled to reach sessions. The Marsh JPs
and Mr Uppleby from Wootton were frequent complainants.

b) High Constables
After the brief hush of the opening ceremonies while the justices
took their places, one of the first important tasks was to 'call
over' the constables. From each wapentake came two or three
high constables who marshalled and led their petty constables,
one from parish, who bore 'wands' (headed and painted staves)
as symbols of office. Together they formed a large contingent.
In Midsummer 1741 at Caistor, from the three wapentakes of
Yarborough, Walshcroft and Bradley Haverstoe, there were in
all five high constables and forty-five petty constables. One of
the constables' duties was to keep order at sessions. Mr John
Raisbeck, high constable of Bradley Haverstoe in 1775, wrote to
the clerk to say that he would not be able to attend the court as
'the piles' made him 'incapable of riding' but as it was the turn
of his constables to 'bear the staffs' he had 'commanded my son
to command my constables to keep good order and see that they
do so'.[5]

High constables held an important office and were usually
men of wealth and standing, such as substantial tenant farmers
or freeholders just below the rank of gentry. They were
appointed by the justices at quarter sessions, usually on the
recommendation of a local magistrate, sometimes on the

suggestion of the last high constable. The high constable of Yarborough wrote to sessions:

> I freely resign the place of Chief Constable.
> You please to make choice of the bearer my
> nephew Hudson will much oblige
> your most obt hble servt
> Parce Teale
> He hath waited of Mr Uppleby.[6]

Uppleby was the local JP. There are several similar letters, but this one catches some significant points. The slightly peremptory tone was possible because it could be difficult to find men to carry out the duties. On the other hand, some men and families seem to have drawn considerable status from the post and retained it for many years. Percival Teale of Immingham, who wrote the letter above, had held office for over thirty years and we find others only retiring when 'age and infirmity' rendered them 'unable to do the business'. Some of them like Henry Newstead of Louth Eske or Chipsey Hornsby at Caistor, were familiar and respected men in the world of sessions. Of course there were black sheep. During the Christmas season of 1763 a raid by the constables of Lincoln 'found Wade Morris, Chief Constable of Aslacoe, in a House of ill fame in the Bail of Lincoln'.[7]

The high constables often acted as the executive officers of quarter sessions. For example, during the great cattle plague of 1747 they transmitted the orders of the magistrates to the parish officers.[8] Later they were asked 'to make returns to certain questions regarding the state of the poor'.[9]

They also supervised and coordinated the work of the petty constables in their wapentakes. Most troublesome and important, they were responsible for two vital tasks. First, they had to ensure that each constable had collected 'the sessions dues' from his parish, the levy 'for defraying the expenses of vagrants, soldiers and seafaring men wanting subsistence'. Second, they had to make sure that each constable produced his 'freeholders bill', the list of all freeholders in his parish qualified to serve on juries. The sessions records are full of minor threats and fines due to constables' neglect of these duties and the high constables must have found enforcement an endless, frustrating task.

The high constables were also charged with the general oversight of their wapentakes, and at the start of sessions they made presentments of any nuisances. These included a range of misdemeanours: often constables 'not returning their freeholders bills'; once a man 'for carrying a gun not being qualified'.[10] However, the great majority of such presentments were for keeping unlicensed ale-houses. Often in the 1740s there were lists of thirty or forty people from each wapentake presented 'for drawing ale without a licence', all suffering the standard fine of forty shillings.

The high constables did much work out of sessions which is not recorded and, as Peyton says in his study of the system in Kesteven in the late seventeenth century, 'of which little is known'.[11] In the past they had held their own courts, especially concerned with matters like weights and measures and vagrants. They were also supposed to hold meetings with their petty constables to record their presentments for sessions. They often supervised the statute or hiring fairs. The sessions records give only the merest glimpses of such activities, if they were continuing. Certainly the high constables did hold regular meetings because in 1771 it was

> Ordered that the Chief Constables do deliver in at the first General Quarter Sessions at which they are required to attend ... tables of the fees taken by them in the Execution of their Office and accounts of the several meetings held by them annually and on what occasions such meetings are held.[12]

Unfortunately the returns have not survived. There is one mention of 'Statute Sessions' in 1772.[13]

At Easter 1743, a high constable presented two of his parish constables 'for not paying for their Presentments bill writing', so perhaps this was the business at the meetings. However, in later years this work was done at the start of sessions, and there are no more clues to tell us what went on.[14]

c) Petty Constables

There is much more to be discovered about the petty constables because their annual accounts often survive. Technically, they were officers of the old manor courts. In 1750 Edward Chambers was elected constable of Sudbrooke 'by the jurors ... at a Court Leet and Court Baron of the Dean and Chapter of Peterborough'.[15] However, by the eighteenth century many of these courts were defunct and in practice it was a matter of each parish having its own customs to persuade one of its male inhabitants to undertake the tedious, perhaps dangerous, duties of constable for a year. Those duties were well described in the oath of office which had to be sworn before a justice:

> You shall duly exercise your office of Constable of the townshipp of A, and well and truly present all mannour of bloodsheddes, assaultes, and affreys and outrages there done and comytted against the Kinges Majesty's peace: All manner of writtes, warrantes and preceptes to you lawfully directed you shall truly execute: the Kinges Majesty's peace in your own person you shall conserve and keepe as much as in you lyeth: And in all other thinges that apperteyne to your office you shall well and truly behave yourself. So help you God and the contentes etc.[16]

A man shouldering such tasks for his neighbours, unpaid, could afford to be a little selective in choosing which duties he carried out. The practice was colourfully expressed by Obediah Midgeley, who submitted the following accounts 'being Cunstable for the Parish of Willoughton this present year 1757'[17] :

	£	s	d
Paid for 2 warnds to Put in insesers of the land tax		2	0
My own charges at the same time at Lincoln		2	6
For going to Lincoln to get the dubly cats sind		2	6
Spent when the accounts wass given hupp		2	6
Two leoads of theoarns for the comon fenses		2	0

Two leoads of staons for Lincoln gate & bainfurs Wall	2	0
Paid to thos post for mending then Walls	3	4
Paid to John hauley & John Banestr for mending comon fences	6	8
Paid to John hauley for cuting a grip to let Water out of clapit yateshead & for feting theoarns for the comon fences	2	4
Paid Thos andrew for Digingstones 5 days	4	2
Paid to Bentouler for Diging stoanes 2 days	1	8
Paid to Will Draton for digin stones 1 Day & a pees	1	0
Paid to John Turner for Digin stones 2 Dayes	1	8
Paid to John Midleton for mending nu spring	1	6
Paid to John Turner for sarveing of him		10
Paid to Joh Turner for dressing the beck beter & the nu spring	4	0
Paid to Will Sauel for diging Stones 4 days	3	4
Paid to Mr Codd for the sise bills	1	8
My own charges at spittle at that time	1	2
Paid to the burleymen for gaps		6
For 3 warnds & ahewncry carring to blibor & 1 to hemsuel		5
Paid to John banester For 2 Days ackinruts in	2	8
For 1 warnd carring to blibor		1
Paid to James Good for diging stones 3 dayes	2	6
Paid to Mr Codd an audermoney deu to the tresery	12	10
My own charges at spittle at that time	1	2
Paid to John Parkinson for tenting beas out of the north field & for making 2 dems in the becks	1	8
For carreying a stoup & some yate ledges to the Ingleys yate & whon to the new Paster	1	0
Paid to Josephmurr	14	10
Paid to the blacksmith	1	9
Paid to John Fairwether for lownces	18	7
Paid to William Pant	7	1
Paid to the burleymen for gapes		6
Paid to the burleymen	7	0
For reighting	1	0

Mr Midgeley's 'reighting' reveals that the tradition of being a manorial officer was still alive in the general supervision of fences, walls, tracks, watercourses and the other manor court officers, the 'burleymen'. His duties as a rating officer are there in the journeys to Lincoln about the land tax and the making of his accounts. The criminal business which is normally associated with constables only appears in his hue and cry and his warrants served at Bliborough and Hemswell. Victorian reformers liked to see the old parish constables as quaint, part-time, inefficient policemen. This was to take particular view for propaganda purposes. The eighteenth-century constables never tried to be policemen in the modern sense; rather, they were the legal executive officers of the manor, the parish, and the justices, and their struggles with their 'reighting' show that, by and large, they did the job adequately.

There are many examples of the problems of the work in the sessions records. Constables frequently had to prosecute householders who 'have not paid their constable's rate'. Occasionally there were actions against people who had refused to help the constable arrest a belligerent suspect. In 1778 nine men from Bardney violently rescued a prisoner from the custody of two constables.[18] In 1774, 'The Constables of Glanford Brigg were violently beaten and assaulted by Wm Barnard, ... butcher, as they were executing a warrant he did take the warrant out of their hands.'[19] There was often trouble in bastardy cases, when constables had to haul those suddenly accused of paternity before the justice. In 1750 the two constables of Stallingborough were each fined fifty shillings for allowing such a father to escape.[20]

No doubt these brief records often conceal sizable affrays, but it seems to have been rare for the constables to flinch. The Horncastle constables once refused to serve a warrant for assault, but the families involved were so well-known for quarrelling and violence that the magistrates did nothing.[21] Otherwise, the actions against constables were 'for not returning their freeholders' bills'. In spite of the difficulty and unpopularity of the office there are only two recorded cases of men refusing to serve. Edward Chambers was fined ten shillings for refusing to be constable of Sudbrooke in 1750 and in 1756

Francis Boone refused to act as constable of Corringham, but the magistrates must have thought he had better reason for he was only fined sixpence.[22]

In the 1740s all constables had to attend quarter sessions, which meant a journey to the local town four times each year. On arrival they were assembled in their wapentakes by their high constables and 'called over' and required to 'answer to their names'. Then they had to make presentments of any nuisances and misdemeanour in their parishes. There was a strong traditional and communal element in this. The constables, as ancient officers of the manor, usually presented offences against the open-field system of farming: pound breach, not maintaining fences, trespass on the common and so on. They also brought actions against those who offended the community's sense of economic justice by engrossing or forestalling goods. The constables also acted against disorderly houses and troublesome ale-houses because a private citizen who had to live next door to such places risked even greater trouble if he prosecuted. In all these cases constables prosecuted in the name of the community, filling the gaps which a system of private actions could not cover.

d) Juries

The constables also had an important part to play in the juries, and it will be convenient to deal with juries at this stage. Constables drew up lists of freeholders in their parishes and from these lists the sheriff's officers, the bailiffs, summoned jurors. For the criminal trials, two juries were required for each sessions: a grand jury to make a preliminary investigation of the indictment and evidence to see if there was a case to answer; and a petty jury, the trial jury which decided the guilt or innocence of the accused.

Much more trouble seems to have been taken over the grand jury. Twenty-four of the more substantial - although not very substantial - freeholders were called, but often only fifteen or sixteen attended. It was customary to describe them simply as 'gent.', but the grand jury list at Caistor for Epiphany 1775 gives more precise information: nine 'gentlemen', one yeoman, one tanner, one brazier, one gardener, one joiner and a carpenter.[23]

The grand jury often made presentments of major local problems, such as unsafe bridges, extortionate ferry charges or the houses of correction being out of repair. Individual grand jurymen presented all sorts of matters, from 'ploughing the town's ground' to being 'a Tear heckler without serving a proper apprenticeship'.

With the petty jury certain shifts, expedients, and quaint rural customs were necessary. In the countryside it was difficult, cumbersome and expensive to summon the right number of jurors to sessions so they simply used the petty constables, usually selecting two or three from each wapentake. In the 1740s it was not uncommon for trial juries to be almost entirely made up from the constables. For example, when Jesse Foster was tried at Caistor Epiphany sessions in 1741 for stealing a rope, ten of the petty jury were constables.[24]

The whole system of juries caused endless trouble. The bailiffs had to rely on lists of freeholders supplied by the constables and sometimes these were deficient. As sheriff's officers, the bailiffs were not under the direct control of the magistrates and this seems to have generated a certain tension. There are several examples of inefficiency or corruption by bailiffs. In 1742 one was fined forty shillings 'for taking a shilling and a pint of port wine' for excusing a juror from attending.[25] Another endorsed his jury list: 'Four of these were summoned, but I really forget who they were.'[26]

The bailiffs had a thankless task, because the freeholders were often recalcitrant. One wrote:

> Sir,
> I should be greatly oblig'd to you to excuse my serving on the jury today and let me be put on for the next sessions in lieu of it. I am sorry to take the freedom with you, but I have a good deal of Company and would not willingly leave them.
> Wm Holgate.[27]

Apart from the tone and the weakness of the excuse, the key point is 'today'. It was this sort of letter that led the bailiffs to shifts like 'Ould Smith not to be found, but junior will appear.'[28]

As well as the difficulties of summoning jurors there was the simple but serious problem that in a rural area like Lindsey there were comparatively few men who qualified to serve by the ownership of land worth forty shillings. Thus freeholders had to do duty frequently: it was common to serve once every two years. There were obvious dangers in such a system, but it was yet another example of the active citizenship of the eighteenth century and it did mean that jurors knew the procedures of the court well, so business could be despatched rapidly.

e) Criminal Trials

Once the proceedings began things happened very quickly. The assembly of the magistrates and clerks, the appearance of the high and petty constables, the swearing in of the grand jurors, all seemed to happen at once, with a few presentments thrown in for good measure. The clerks prepared the indictments while these preliminaries were taking place.[29] These were forms on parchment with blanks for dates, names, places and crimes to be filled in. The names of prosecutors and witnesses were written at the bottom. They seem to have been written hurriedly in open court and they are obviously the result of verbal interrogation. The clerks wrote down what they thought they heard: dates are usually given as the first of the month; names are mis-spelt; occupations are generalised; places of residence and places where the crimes were committed are mixed casually. In rural Lindsey it did not seem to matter. There were only two instances of cases being quashed on the grounds 'indictment not sufficient' in the whole period 1740 to 1780.

The same rapid informality prevailed when the indictments were carried to the grand jury. At Spilsby, they seem to have met in the corner of the court-room: 'Ordered that the Treasurer of this Sessions take a place in the South West Corner of the Town's Hall for the privacy of the Grand Jury.' At Horncastle they had a private room, but apparently they stood up, until it was ordered 'that benches and a Table be made in the Grand Jury Chamber in the Sessions Hall at Horncastle'.[30]

After a rapid consideration of the evidence, if the grand jurors thought it insufficient they endorsed the indictment 'No Bill' and the prisoner was discharged. If they thought there was a case to answer the indictment was marked 'A True Bill' and the prosecution continued. In spite of the haste, this was no mere formality. The grand jury was a vital part of the system. Its purpose was to protect citizens from malicious prosecutions, especially from tyrannical proceedings by those of greater power or wealth. No man might be tried until a jury of his peers was satisfied that there was a case to answer. It was common belief in the eighteenth century that Englishmen enjoyed greater liberty under the law than foreigners labouring under absolute kings. The grand jury was one justification for such claims and in the 1740s it was still vigorous. Although the Lindsey records are incomplete, it seems that something between one-fifth and one-quarter of all indictments were thrown out by the grand jury.

Of what happened next we know very little indeed, for the minutes and rolls do not give details of trial procedures. We can only infer from the sense of the documents and better-recorded practice elsewhere. When a prisoner pleaded 'not guilty' he could elect to be tried immediately or he could choose to 'traverse'. This usually meant postponement to a future date, giving time to prepare a defence, consult a solicitor, and the right to challenge the indictment. Most elected to be tried immediately.

The eighteenth-century trial was very different from a modern one. The case opened with the prosecutor telling his story and his witnesses supporting him. The magistrates and the jury took an active part, interrupting to ask questions. The defendant was allowed to cross examine and give his version. The key differences from modern practice were that the prisoner was not assumed to be innocent until proven guilty and there was no conception of scientific proof, no notion of deciding guilt or innocence by dispassionate calculation of the facts. The eighteenth-century approach was that there was a case to answer and the weight of that case was very important. An accusation supported by a single witness was unlikely to succeed; one supported by many was unlikely to fail. In reaching a verdict the character, the personality and the attitude of the accused were vital. The jury wanted to form a judgement of the accused as a person and to assess whether the prosecution case was likely to be correct. It was a human, intuitive judgement, not a mechanical one. This explains why the magistrates liked to send explanatory notes with their recognizances, why the jurors and magistrates took such an active part in trials and why character references could be so important. When William Stothard shot a bay mare sixteen of his fellow-parishioners wrote to the court:

> Worthy Gentlemen,
>   We ... do certify that Wm Stothard is a person honest and industrious, and has a large family and that we never knew him guilty of any flagrant crime, and we firmly believe that he is entirely innocent of what he is now accused, and that the misfortune was purely accidental; wherefore we earnestly and heartily intreat you to consider the poor man's case with clemency and commiseration.[31]

The old attitude also explains why the use of lawyers was discouraged. They came between the jury and the man, screening the reality by clever tricks and deceptions. What need of a lawyer had an honest man? For these reasons lawyers had been barred from most criminal trials in the late seventeenth century, but by the 1720s the prohibition was weakening and lawyers were being used in London at assizes. However, it took many years for this practice to filter down to rural quarter sessions in Lindsey. Of course, there were always plenty of lawyers about: Mr Jollands, Mr Saunderson, Mr Knight, Mr Bernard, Mr Hildyard and the rest were all familiar figures at sessions. They were invariably used in settlement cases, when two parishes argued out which one was responsible for a pauper. But this was quite different from a criminal trial: the points at issue were technical and legal, not human, judgements. For the same reason lawyers were often used in disputes about the possession of land.

Edging beyond such technical cases, lawyers were sometimes employed by busy farmers or gentry to plead guilty in nuisance cases. For example, an attorney appeared on behalf of Mr West of Saltfleetby to accept that his client had 'blocked the road with a cart of manure'. No doubt the shilling fine was the least of Mr West's charges.[32] If a client could afford it and the case depended largely on technical matters, perhaps in a trespass, then again a solicitor might be engaged. The court itself, or other official bodies, might use a lawyer to bring an action: Mr Jollands was employed to prosecute the keeper of the house of correction for discharging a prisoner without authority.[33] The limits of lawyers' involvement in criminal trials came when the accused chose to traverse. Then, especially if he was wealthy, he would undoubtedly seek advice in preparing his case. He might, although there is no written evidence of this in the Lindsey records, have his solicitor near him in the court to give further advice during the trial. However, the balance of the evidence seems to be against such practice in the 1740s. The presence of a lawyer would be counter-productive, implying that there was something to hide, or that greater wealth was being used to buy a favourable verdict.

As with the use of lawyers, there is little concrete evidence about what happened once verdicts were given. According to Peyton, in Kesteven the usual practice was to hear the cases, and then adjourn for dinner. After dinner the justices took administrative business and then returned to the court to pass sentences. This may have happened in Lindsey and the casual recording of sentences supports the idea: often they were only recorded as footnotes to the indictments or not at all. On the other hand the trials must have gone on at a cracking pace and, because sessions were adjourned to several places, the magistrates liked to complete the business in one day, if possible. They aimed to finish criminal proceedings in the morning or early part of the afternoon and then the justices adjourned to the White Hart, the Ship, or some suitable inn to eat and deal with administrative matters. However, criminal business commonly over-ran, and did not finish until three, four, or even five p.m.. In these circumstances it seems likely that judgement was given in the formal atmosphere of the court before adjourning. Perhaps on those uncomfortable occasions when weight of business forced them to return to the sessions hall for a second morning they may have reserved some sentences until that time. Those found not guilty were 'discharged by proclamation'.

f)   Punishment

Many crimes were resolved without punishment because they never came before the courts. There were many forms of informal social control which might be used. Some of the earliest petty sessions minutes for Lindsey, for Bradley Haverstoe wapentake in the 1830s, record instructions from the bench to local employers asking them to mediate between or control their labourers: 'a note to be written to Mr Coates requesting him to endeavour to keep the peace between the parties, they being the wife and daughter of two of his labourers'; or again, about a man who had assaulted a girl: 'a note to Mr Francis to speak to his shepherd'.[34] Although there are no such notes in the eighteenth-century quarter sessions records it seems most likely that such practices were widespread.

Sometimes the local community dealt with offenders in its own way, although only a tiny number of such incidents ended in court proceedings. Much village intrigue and riot probably lay behind the prosecution of John Wells of Osgodby who in 1751, 'wrote, published, and did fix to the wall' of a neighbour's house a paper bearing the classic verse:

> Horns, Horns upon my Door,
> I am a cuckold and my wife a whore.
> If any can against it say,
> Take these cuckold's horns away.[35]

Even when cases did come before the courts many did not end in punishment in a modern sense. One of the most common solutions to minor disputes was the device of binding to keep the peace. This meant that someone accused of threatening another's person or property had to promise to keep the king's peace, and had to find two neighbours who would stand sureties, usually of £20 or £40. In fact, this simple and popular procedure had many complex applications and variations, but it was most often used to settle assaults. Three hundred of the 700 assault cases were resolved by some version of binding over. All those so bound had to attend sessions but then there were several different possibilities. In 100 cases the bench ordered the binding over be continued. Many of the other 200 cases do not have a clear outcome because informal procedures were used.

Often the prosecutors had rushed before a magistrate in the heat of argument, but later repented and withdrew, or perhaps witnesses refused to appear. Justice Harrison sent a note when Elizabeth Adam was accused of stealing from Richard Nelthorpe: 'Mr Marshall, Mr Nelthorpe's steward may be called if they prosecute ... if not, she may be discharged'.[36] Such practices were not only very confusing for future historians who want to know what all the odd recognizances were for, they were also illegal. In law no prosecutor, no magistrate, could leave matters like this; it was not up to them. The king's peace had been broken and proper restitution, according to law, must be concluded by the courts. Unfortunately, as Dalton had regretted as long ago as 1661 'the usage now is and long hath been to the contrary'.[37]

Many cases were settled by arbitration. On 25 August 1741 Mary Harrison of Lincoln claimed Richard Pearson had assaulted her. Pearson was bound in £50 to appear at Michaelmas sessions. However, the bond is endorsed: 'On 1st October 1741 Mary Harrison came before Chancellor Reynolds and released Richard Pearson from this recognizance'.[38] More commonly such cases were simply marked 'Agreed', but there are a few letters which give more details of the process. Some are brief and casual: 'Note to Mr John - Pray these few lines is to satisfy the court that you and I have agreed - From your humble servant John Oxey.'[39] Some are more respectful:

> These are to certify your worships that I have agreed with my Master Wightman the Sessions affair, and the charges to be paid equally between my master and me and allso allow myself in fault as a witness.
> Wm Walker
> Tested Ed Cottrell.[40]

Others record a much more formal process of arbitration: 'Agreed between solicitors of parties that all matters between them be referred to Thos Hardy of Louth, Doctor of Physick.' [41]

Hardy was an active magistrate. Three labourers in an assault case agreed that 'the matter of dispute between them be put to Edward Eastland and George Goodhelp, and if they don't agree to a third whose determination shall be final'. There followed a complicated division of costs. [42]

Beyond arbitration and binding over the most common punishment for minor offences, especially for assault, was a fine. The 'standard rate' was sixpence. However, if the magistrates thought the offence was particularly severe they might impose a fine of a few pounds and this was usually a far more severe punishment than it appeared. As few ordinary people could afford such sums they were detained in the house of correction 'until payment', which meant until the magistrate, or perhaps the prosecutor, saw fit to release them. Something of the personal effect of such a sentence is revealed in James Carmichael's letter. In May 1746 Carmichael, an ex-soldier, got into a fight in a pub in Kirton. He assaulted the landlord 'and dangerously threatened his dwelling-house, and said that he would make it black in a little time', which the magistrates took to mean that he would fire it. They took serious view of the threat, fined him £5 and sent him to Lincoln Castle 'until payment'. The horrors of that place and the uncertainty of release drew this letter from Carmichael six months later:

> May it please your worships,
> The Petition of James Carmical now in the Gaol of Lincoln now confined for the sum of £5 ... he haveing been in confinement ever since May last being a poor wounded soldier and discharged out of Borril's Regiment at York haveing no place of settlement for his poor wife big with child and three small children to maintain and forced to sell her clothes for to buy them provisions and now all ready to starve for succour.
> Hopeing your worships will pitty our deplorable condition and grant relief. Therefore your poor petitioner with very great submission humbly requests the great favour of your worships to be pleased to take of his fine and discharge him

from his confinement.
    For the sake of his poor family in order to
their subsistence,
            James Carmical, his mark.[43]

There is no record of what happened to Carmichael, but the usual practice was to mitigate the fine to sixpence and release the prisoner.

Fines were rarely used to punish theft. Of 153 people convicted of theft between 1740 and 1780 only fourteen were fined and of those only ten escaped with the small sixpenny fines commonly handed down for assaults. One hundred and twenty-one or about eighty per cent of those convicted of theft were ordered to be flogged 'until the body be bloody'. These floggings were carried out by the keepers of the houses of correction and the standard sentence seems to have been twenty lashes. However, there were variations and the magistrates gave precise instructions, apparently trying to vary the flogging to fit the crime. The most lenient sentence was to be whipped 'privately'; on one occasion they even ordered that an old lady be 'whipp'd gently'.[44]

Sometimes floggings were combined with a brief spell in the house of correction to add fear and the opportunity for reflection to the sentence. When Martha Hand stole five pounds of bacon she was ordered to be 'committed to the House of Correction for one night, privately whipped tomorrow morning and discharged'.[45] Most floggings were carried out publicly. Again, the time and place were varied: they could be 'at the door of the House of Correction', or 'at the rising of the court'. Often it was thought worthwhile to show justice done in the place where the offence had been committed. Thus Ann Scoffin, convicted of stealing 'ten ears of wheat in the sheaves valued at one penny' was to be 'committed till Saturday next, then conveyed to Barton and whipped next market day'.[46]

Sometimes the floggings were carefully prescribed, as if after some sort of nice calculation to give maximum fear, humiliation, and pain to the convict, revenge to the victim, and example to the community. Elizabeth Leaning, who stole some cloth from a shop in Barton, was

> To remain in the custody of the Constable of
> Barton till Monday next, then to be whipped naked
> from the waiste upwards ty'd to a cart, and
> whipped publicly in time of full market from the
> sign of the George to the house of Thomas
> Sherlock in Barton till her body be bloody.[47]

Cruder severity was ordered in very few cases, but Daniel
Paddison was

> committed to the House of Correction for three
> months and to be kept to hard labour; to be taken
> out and whipped publicly by the master of the
> House once a month on Louth market day between
> the hours of 11 a.m. and 2 p.m., and not to be
> discharged until he finds sureties for good
> behaviour.[48]

Such a sentence reflected the outrage of the bench at
Paddison's offence: he had felled a tree in one of the
magistrates' new parks.

The houses of correction were mainly used for vagrants and
for those awaiting trial who were remanded in custody because it
was feared they would escape (for example fathers in bastardy
cases), or be a danger to other people (for example men accused
of violence towards their families). The house of correction was
rarely used to punish convicts. Only seven, less than five per
cent, of those found guilty of theft were sent to the house.
Terms were brief: usually one or three months, occasionally six.
The record was held by William Paddison, sentenced to two
years 'for mayhemming his wife'.[49] However, even a short stay
in the houses must have been a very unpleasant experience.

After 1742 there were two houses of correction in Lindsey:
one at Gainsborough and one at Louth. They were small and
usually each held only about a dozen prisoners. Both seem to
have been neglected and poorly maintained. The grand jury
described the 'dwelling house' at Louth as 'ruinous and very
much out of repair'; the garden 'very ruinous and decay'd'; and
warned that 'the walls of the yard are insufficient to secure the

prisoners'.[50] At Gainsborough, 'the out door near the yard and the windows of the working shop' were 'insufficient'; 'a new strong door and frame should be added to the Prison'; and 'cross iron bars should be added to the prison windows'.[51] These ramshackle structures were not secure, and escapes were common. The unfortunate keeper of Gainsborough had to report two at Epiphany sessions 1756: 'John Smith escaped on 6 September', and 'Thomas Wood made his escape out of the prison on January 11'. One night in 1777 he had to move all the prisoners out of the 'low cell' to prevent them 'getting out by letting down the frame of the window'.[52] Conditions were primitive. The main prison rooms in both houses were condemned as 'damp and unhealthy'.[53] At night, the prisoners lay on straw. Some were kept in irons: 'Fetters reviting on, one shilling'. At Louth, a 'strong post' was 'set down in the middle of the room' and prisoners were chained to it at night. Those sentenced to hard labour were 'employed in teezing old rope into Ockham for caulking ships and other vessels', or pounding bricks into dust. Some of the vagrants also suffered 'moderate correction weekly': 'By cash for beating Kemp, four shillings and sixpence'.[54]

Prisoners accused of serious offences, awaiting delivery at assizes, were sent to the county gaol at Lincoln. That place, with its 'horrid dungeon', the 'foul pit' where the condemned were held, was probably worse than the houses of correction, but the castle surgeon's report gives a fair impression of the varieties of human misery that lay on the straw at Gainsborough and Louth each night:

> P.Parnell, Surgeon. Lincoln, October 6 1788.
> A Report of the Patients, Debtors and Felons since Midsummer and this Michaelmas Sessions in the Castle of Lincoln.

Bottomley	A bilious fever	Cured
Chevins	A bilious fever	Cured
Drewry	Ulcerated sore throat	Cured
Several felons	The Itch	Cured
A felon man	Venereal	Cured
Wilkinson	A remittent fever	Cured

Rase	A spasmodick complaint	Cured
Scarborough	A pain in her head	Cured
Wilcock	Hystericks	Cured
Hitchcock	Dropsical	Cured
Shaw	A Pleumetical fever	Cured

Mr Parnell concluded that they were 'At present all tolerably well'.[55]

The most serious punishment that could be inflicted at quarter sessions was transportation, but it was rarely used. Only nineteen people were 'ordered to be transported to His Majesty's colonies in America' from Lindsey between 1740 and 1780. In seventeen of the cases the crime was theft and the sentence seven years. The two others were convicted of receiving stolen goods and sentenced to fourteen years. Some of the crimes were grand larceny, involving considerable quantities of goods, so the prisoners may have thought themselves lucky to be tried at sessions and transported: they might have faced the death penalty at assizes. Occasionally there are hints that those selected for transportation were regarded as 'professional' criminals: John Laughton was convicted of three separate thefts; Mary Mead was described as 'a pick pocket'.[56]

Finally, there were some idiosyncratic punishments. Two of the eight women convicted of keeping brothels between 1740 and 1780 were ordered to stand in the pillory, one for half-an-hour, one for an hour. This seems to have been a punishment reserved exclusively for this offence, and applied only to females in the larger towns of Gainsborough and Lincoln.[57]

Samuel Cooper, convicted of stealing ten traps in 1788, was sentenced to three years in the house of correction, and to be publicly whipped on some two market days at Gainsborough, 'unless he shall sooner enter into some regiment going to the East Indies or into the Honourable East India Company's service'.[58]

g) The Strength of the System in the 1740s
At this stage, having sketched the main types of crime in rural Lindsey, and described the means of controlling it, it is possible

to examine the strength of the system in the 1740s, and to answer the original question, 'Why did the crime rate fall?'. The next chapter will show that this was partly caused by changes in the administration of the courts but nevertheless, there was a real downward trend and there was a feeling that crime was under control. How could a system of half a dozen active magistrates without any modern police force be so successful in governing such a violent and rumbustious society?

The answer is not to be found in the use of terror. Naturally the serious crimes and hangings of the assizes were well-recorded and have come to dominate much folklore and popular history, but they were only a very small part of the system at the time. In Lindsey in the 1770s at most fifteen per cent of accused were sent for trial at assizes; of those, only about half were found guilty and only a quarter of these convicts were sentenced to death. Probably half of the condemned were reprieved. Thus, out of nearly 600 people before the courts in the 1770s only about six were executed.[59] In a brutal age half a dozen executions in a decade is slender evidence for a regime of terror based on a 'bloody code'.

The macabre theatre of assizes tried to express not terror, but the majesty of the law. To an illiterate and superstitious society the elaborate ceremonial and the death penalty were intended to convey the notion that English law was not just a jumble of human expedients but a reflection of 'natural law', a higher system which thus claimed the right of life and death over all. More prosaically, the presence of the king's judges confirmed that the law administered in rural Lindsey was part of a national system; that what the magistrates decreed in the hired schoolroom in Louth next Tuesday was not an arbitrary ruling but justice governed by a greater authority.

Correspondingly, the success of the local magistrates did not rest on terror. First, there were not enough of them: the usual six or so active magistrates would have found it hard to terrorise an area the size of Lindsey. Secondly, they were not the petty tyrants of fiction; most seem to have been decent, hard-working men, motivated by a sense of duty. Thirdly, they lacked the fear which drives tyranny. Certainly they hunted down Jacobites, were suspicious of papists and feared riots in an unstable age, but they did not bring these fears to sessions. The antiquarian William Stukely (1687-1765) was a Lincolnshire magistrate for the Parts of Holland, and his doggerel about quarter sessions catches the attitude of the justices.

> Three or four parsons, Three or four squires,
> Three or four lawyers, three or four lyers,
> Three or four parishes bringing appeals,
> Three or four hands and three or four seals.
> Three or four statutes not understood,
> Three or four paupers praying for food,
> Three or four roads that never were mended,
> Three or four scolds - the Sessions is ended.[60]

It is not only Stukely's attitude which denies tyranny. He illustrates another significant factor. At assizes about sixty per cent of cases were offences against property, and it is easy to build a structure of class oppression on this base. At quarter sessions much of the business was not what we would call crime at all. In Lindsey in the 1740s, all offences against property (theft, fraud, receiving, poaching) made up only sixteen per cent of all cases heard at sessions. Over half the actions at sessions concerned local government and administration: ten per cent prosecution of those who failed to perform parish duties or maintain roads; fifteen per cent control of ale-houses; nearly twenty-five per cent poor law cases, including vagrancy and enrolling bastardy bonds. It must be emphasised that these were prosecutions; much further administrative business, such as confirmation of appointments, checking accounts and finance, did not require legal action, but took up a great deal of time after dinner at the inn.

Many actions arose from petty disputes which required arbitration rather than punishment. Arguments produced by the complexities of open-field farming provided ten per cent of the business. Assaults were the largest single category of offences at twenty per cent of the whole. Most were trivial, resolved by arbitration, binding over or sixpenny fines. Even the thefts posed no threat to the social order: most involved tiny items, snatched on impulse. For the magistrates it was tiresome rather than threatening.

Stukely's boredom reminds us that the magistrates did not initiate actions and that the whole system was driven by private prosecutions. In assaults most of the prosecutors were poor, the social equals of the accused; in thefts, most were small tradesmen, craftsmen and farmers; most administrative actions were brought by parish officers. Why were they all so willing to prosecute? Often the matters were trivial. Prosecutors were not paid for their trouble and as convicts were usually poor there was very little hope of costs or compensation. A case at sessions required fees for warrants, expenses for witnesses, time away from work, difficult journeys and considerable nerve, organisation and determination. Yet poor people, ordinary people, did prosecute; in a significant minority of cases even vulnerable people, like battered wives and servants or paupers unjustly treated by parish officers, took their oppressors to sessions. Why? And how could such a system work?

One factor was the idea of the king's peace, a perfect standard which it was the duty of all citizens to uphold. This fostered the notion of an active citizenship, and enabled the system to work without a large bureaucracy. It also allowed the magistrates to stiffen prosecutors' resolve. Once a breach of the king's peace was reported to a magistrate he might bind the prosecutor to act; although in practice such demands were often waived if the breach was healed in reality.

The king's peace was supported by a powerful sense of community. Such an idea is controversial. Professor Holmes argues that it is very difficult to see late seventeenth-century Lincolnshire villages as strong communities when there was clearly a great deal of migration and commercial pressures were changing agriculture.[61] On the other hand, it is common to associate the idea of community with a romantic, cosy picture of village life in the past. The sessions records emphatically contradict this: life was hard and often brutal. Nevertheless, there was a real sense of community in most Lindsey villages in the eighteenth century. The village was the unit of production: all those who lived in the village worked in the village. Moreover, where the open fields still existed, farmers and labourers had to co-operate. The village was still the most important unit of government, controlling roads, crime and a whole range of 'social services'. The village church was still an important centre for consultation, and for celebrating the 'rites of passage'. Thus even if there was migration, even if a man moved, he was quickly forced to fit into the economy, government and society of his new village. The community structure was essential and powerful.

It is easy to forget just how small Lindsey villages were in the eighteenth century: most contained only thirty or forty families, around 150 people in all. Many were smaller, with less than 100 inhabitants and even the larger settlements, with perhaps 450 residents, were insignificant hamlets by today's standards. This strengthened the community because it encouraged a sense of commonwealth. In a small community it was easier to appreciate the consequences of actions or omissions. An extra vagrant or illegitimate child meant a real increase in village poor rates; neighbours would force the overseer to act. A farmer who ignored the customs of the open fields offended not one, but many of the residents; they quickly combined to make him mend his fences or move his pile of muck. They were encouraged to do so by traditions of the manor court and communal mechanisms like the field juries. Crime was much more likely to upset the whole community. If something was stolen, the victim could often guess the culprit and, of course, stolen items were difficult to conceal. A gang of neighbours quickly assembled, called out the constable and challenged the suspect. Their presence created a momentum which carried the proceedings beyond the angry exchange in the village, up to the magistrate's house and eventually to sessions. In this way, in a small village the community created strong pressure to prosecute. To allow the culprit to go unpunished was a clear neglect of duty before the whole parish. Often it must have been easier to follow the traditional path and prosecute.

Finally, people used the courts because it was unavoidable. No-one wished to bring unnecessary actions because magistrates, parish officers, prosecutors and witnesses were all unpaid, and all had much other work to do. Very few had the time or money to bring frivolous or simply vindictive prosecutions. But the law was an essential part of many aspects of ordinary life: the complex system of farming the open-fields simply could not operate without the law; without the law the poor law could not be administered; markets could not function justly; servants bound to live with masters could not be protected; the spontaneous violence of the pubs and streets could not be controlled; the small property of tradesmen and craftsmen who always lived close to disaster could not be protected. These necessities had created a tradition of litigation among the ordinary people. In this sense, and again Stukely's rhyme catches the idea, the magistrates were providing a service, not oppressing their inferiors. It would be too egalitarian to talk of the people's law; this was a very unequal society. But it could be described as a system of vernacular justice, because it was deeply traditional, customary, and was driven by the real needs of the people. In the 1740s, it worked.

PART III. THE TRANSFORMATION OF THE SYSTEM 1740-80

6 THE 1740s: THE LAST OF THE OLD SYSTEM

a) Patricians and Barbarians

Between 1740 and 1780 there were major changes in the administration of justice in Lindsey, a shift from 'vernacular justice' to government from above. Perhaps revolution is too strong a term, but certainly the changes in the legal system parallel the much more famous and visible changes which were taking place in the landscape as pattern-book houses replaced vernacular buildings and the open fields were enclosed as part of 'the agricultural revolution'.

   In her study of the justices of the peace in Kent between 1679 and 1760, Norma Landau argues that older 'patriarchal' attitudes were being superseded by more 'patrician' views. 'Patriarchal' she defines as 'action by a superior which the community desires for the defence of its interests, but which can be executed only by a person of uncommon powers'; whereas 'patrician' government is 'action by a superior which the superior realises will benefit the community, though the community may not be mature enough to appreciate the wisdom of the action'. The crucial distinction is that, 'The first demands a leader so affected by the condition of his inferiors that he instantly springs to their defence; the second a leader sufficiently distanced from the community to discern its contours and its path'.[1]

These patrician attitudes dominated the thinking of Lindsey gentlemen by the mid-eighteenth century. They were becoming less divided amongst themselves as the political struggles of the seventeenth century were finally laid to rest, but they were becoming increasingly separated from the people they ruled. It was not just a matter of wealth; the gentry had always been much richer than the poor. In many ways the poor still clung to traditional ways of thought: they had little technology to cushion them from the vagaries of weather, harvests, and disease; many were illiterate. In such circumstances they often made sense of the world through magic, superstition, ceremony, and popular religion. It was their way of controlling what Obelkevich has called 'an animate, polymorphous universe'.[2]

Increasingly the gentlemen were abandoning this traditional, 'mythical thinking', for modern 'critical' thought. They were literate, and used a standard English quite different from Lindsey dialects; they based conclusions on evidence and observation; things which had previously been objects of mystery and reverence became matters for investigation. When the tomb of 'Little Saint Hugh' was opened in Lincoln Cathedral the small skeleton was found encased in a green pickle.[3] Joseph Banks tasted the pickle. They prided themselves as men of reason, masters of a universe which Newton had shown to be governed by laws regular and comprehensible to those of education and sense. The churches they built, like the one at Langton, were places where religion might be understood through reason: plain brick boxes, where the pulpit was much more important than the altar and the font was a small functional dish.

In government, such ideas were strongly reinforced by a growing admiration for the classical world, which can still be seen in so much eighteenth-century architecture. In 1720 some gentlemen of Lincolnshire, including several Lindsey magistrates, went so far as to form 'The Order of Roman Knights', which eulogised Henry VIII because he had cleansed the land of 'those swarms of vermin', the 'cloystered nuns and fryers', who had languished in 'delusion and abominable superstition'. The Order set out to find and illustrate Roman ruins, even though they knew they would face opposition from 'Goths and barbarians'.⁴ The Roman world was a powerful image for magistrates and landowners: austere, masculine and willing to take harsh decisions to control ignorant people who did not understand their greater civilization.

Like the Romans, the eighteenth-century gentry were 'eminently, defiantly, incurably, urban'.⁵ They despised the countryside and its ignorant people. In November 1782 the active justice and member of parliament Robert Vyner wrote to a neighbour from his home at Gautby:

> I am going to London about the meeting of Parliament and mean to steal about three weeks for the Xmas recess, which time I should be glad to spend in Lincolnshire; but Gautby is so dirty and dull at that season that I cannot swallow the Pill immediately upon a return from London, but if it would not be inconvenient to you to lend me your house at Ormsby I could with great pleasure pass the recess there, where I should be in reach of Mr Chaplin and in a neighbourhood of some society.⁶

The sophistication of the city and its society made the country seem dirty and primitive. The people who lived there could be little more than barbarians. A Gainsborough poet expressed such feelings powerfully in 1736:

> The Goths were not so barb'rous a Race,
> As the grim Rusticks of this Motly Place;
> Of Reason void, and Thought; whom Interest rules
> Yet will be Knaves, tho' Nature made them *Fools!*
> A strange half Human and ungainly Brood,
> Their Speech uncouth, as are their Manners rude!⁷

The people were ruled by 'Interest', by instinct; they were incapable of Reason. The plight of a country justice marooned amongst them was described by Burrell Massingberd of South Ormsby. He wrote to a friend:

... who can expect less than that an old woman should presently come, with an 'And please you, zur, hearing you can cast a figure, I whopp you will tell ma whar my quey may be found, that I loost t'uther day'. In short, my dear Mr Allam, unless you help me to a fresh supply of conversation from London (tho it were bottled up I would not care) I shall lose my very English, as well as my witts, for here they talk naught but dagmaferish.[8]

The tone is not unkindly; probably Mr Massingberd did what he could to find the cow and certainly he would have issued warrants and bonds if legal action was required. The few active magistrates had always shouldered such work. But as the distance between them and the poor grew it became increasingly frustrating that the people were prepared to languish in such unnecessary ignorance and poverty. When Viscount Torrington toured Lincolnshire he discussed the terrible condition of the poor one evening in Sibsey churchyard, remarking how many of the headstones recorded premature deaths. The cause, he thought, was ignorance, that the poor 'never understood their own management'.[9] It was a theme which more and more of the gentry repeated, often with irritation. Arthur Young thought the old farming systems 'supine' and 'execrable' in Lincolnshire. Ignorance forced the small farmers to 'work like negroes, and not live as well as the inhabitants of the poor house'. Some of Young's informants put it more harshly: the poor, they said, 'swarmed upon the land', the women 'doing nothing but bring children and eat cake'.[10]

This was the patrician attitude indeed. Surely it was the duty of a gentleman to do something about the ignorance and poverty of the people. Their archaic way of life must be improved. Any protest from the country people could be ignored, because the improvements were for their own good; they were just too primitive to understand. By mid-century a powerful improving spirit was abroad, to rationalise old structures and make them more efficient.

b) Signs of Change

Seventeenth-century Lincolnshire provides support for Landau's thesis of a 'patriarchal' gentry, closely associated with and acting to defend their poorer neighbours. The gentry of the Isle of Axholme and the Fens had led the resistance to drainage and enclosure. As late as 1726, when local people rioted against the removal of the spires from Lincoln cathedral, Mr Kent, sometime mayor of the city, believed 'that the people could rise for twenty miles around in defence of their spires, and that the Gentlemen of the County were for preserving their spires'.[11]

Occasional incidents in the eighteenth-century sessions records might be interpreted as remnants of this 'paternal' attitude. About one-quarter of the active justices 1740-80 came from old-established families. Some of them, like the Langtons, had been established in 'their country' for centuries and were traditionally expected to supervise parish government, resolve local disputes, and administer justice. Sometimes outsiders accused them of favouring 'their people'. When John Harrison gave judgement against a farmer for not paying wages to one of his servants, the farmer retorted, 'that it was hard upon him, and he (Harrison) would not have done so if he had been Harrison's tenant'.[12] The sense of paternalism could be intensified if an ancient family felt beleaguered by its Toryism. The Hickmans of Gainsborough spring to mind. Throughout the period Hickman remained a central figure in any appointments that were made to local offices. In 1779 he wrote that there had been 'many competitors for the appointment of the chief constable of Corringham wapentake' and that the matter 'had greatly engaged my attention, to enquire the merits of each'. He had finally decided to recommend Mr Thomas Hill of Scotter, because he was supported by 'so many persons of worth and significance'.[13]

But that letter is headed 'Thonock Grove'. The Hickmans had abandoned their ancient home, the 'Old Hall', in the middle of Gainsborough. A new classical mansion, a 'sylvan seat', had been built a few miles north of the town. Throughout the county, gentlemen were building afresh or improving old houses and surrounding them with landscaped parks. This separation from their people was more than symbolic. It became physically more daunting to approach the new country mansion, some miles from the village, set in a large park and staffed with gatekeepers, butlers and clerks, who had to be negotiated before the magistrate could be reached. In 1762 Thomas Showler was appointed overseer of the poor for the parish of Haugh. He wanted to appeal against the appointment, but found it very difficult to do so. He wrote out four copies of the grounds of his appeal and on 2 July set off to walk or ride the two miles to the nearest magistrate, Mr Dashwood of Well Vale. There 'two copys I laid upon they table in the servants' hall ... Mr Dashwood refueseing to admit me near him, and also the Butler said that Mr Dashwood would have nothing to do with me.' He then rode four miles to the Massingberd's at Ormsby, where

> the same day I delivered two copys to Ann Farrow, servt to Mr Burrell Massingberd at Ormsby, who said her master was gone on a journey and would not be at home in a week's time, and as soon as he got home she would deliver the same to him, and I acquainted her with the contents of the notices.[14]

In other small but perceptible ways the administration of justice was becoming more formal, perhaps with signs that magistrates were losing personal knowledge of the people they governed. High constables' presentments at sessions were changing. In the early 1740s they regularly presented a range of misdemeanours in their wapentakes but soon the only offence they presented was 'drawing ale without a licence', for which there was a standard fine of forty shillings. But the great lists of thirty or forty people so presented appear suspect and artificial in some ways. They are spasmodic, as if in response to prodding from higher authority: in some years there are few, in others many. They seem to have been hurriedly drafted, as if to prove that the high constables were active, rather than showing real concern for a genuine problem. Often the names of those accused have been marked by the clerk 'does not draw', or even, 'no such person'.[15]

Petty constables' presentments were declining even more. In the early 1740s they still show vigorous action on behalf of those who offended the community with presentments for pound breach, 'fences down', 'trespass on the common' and 'engrossing and forestalling goods'. However, the presentment sheets which the petty constables handed to their high constables rapidly declined to:

> The Presentment of us and every of us whose names are subscribed being Constables of the severall towns hereunder mention'd within Corringham Hundred do declare that wee nor any of us have anything presentable within our severall Constabularies since the last Sessions to the best of our knowledge.

This was verified by eight signatures and two marks. At least such nullity was respectful of traditional forms. Soon this degenerated into sheets headed with the name of the wapentake but with nothing written beneath, or even to the final contempt of scraps of paper with the single word 'nothing' scrawled on them.[16]

Thus even in the 1740s there were the first signs of change: more distance between the magistrates and the people; a decline in the system of constables' presentments. The latter marked a significant weakening of the ability of the community to control those whose petty misdemeanour made life unpleasant for their neighbours. Increasingly, such matters were left to private prosecution.

c)   The Re-organisation of 1749

There was a really sharp change in 1749, which must have brought home to many ordinary people and parish officers the tendency towards a more formal and remote court of quarter sessions. Until this time each sessions had been adjourned to several little towns around the Parts of Lindsey, usually meeting at Gainsborough, Spital, Caistor, Louth, Spilsby, and Horncastle. This was convenient for ordinary people and parish officers, because sessions came to them. Moreover, it probably made the court less daunting. After a short journey to their local and well-known market town they faced a small bench of only two or three equally local and well-known magistrates. However, it was troublesome for the clerk of the peace and some of the senior magistrates whose experience might be required at more than one place, because it meant travelling round the county for at least a week, a cold and uncomfortable business in winter.

In 1749 old Mr Sapsford, who had been clerk of the peace for nearly thirty years, died. He was replaced by Thomas Brackenbury. Brackenbury probably owed his appointment to his close relationship with the lord lieutenant, the duke of Ancaster. The Ancasters had abandoned their home in 'Spilsbyshire' to live closer to London at Grimsthorpe, and Brackenbury had been employed as agent to run the old estates. He was an administrator and attorney of some ability building up a reputation and large practice in Spilsby. In many ways he was representative of the competent eighteenth-century gentleman, keen to run things efficiently and rationally.

There may also have been political motives for change. In London, after the fall of Walpole and the defeat of the Jacobites in 1745, the government was trying to broaden the base of its support. At local level this meant appointing to the bench some Tory gentlemen who had previously been regarded with suspicion and excluded or who had simply been unwilling to serve. In 1745 the Lord Chancellor emphasised the new policy: 'In all Commissions of the Peace, hereafter to be issued, all proper regard shall be had to Gentlemen of Figure and Fortune, well-affected to His Majesty's Government, without Distinction of Parties.'[17] While the rulers of Lindsey were probably in favour of Tory gentlemen taking their share of the work, the current practice of adjourning sessions from place to place made it difficult, or at least uncomfortable. At most such sessions there were only two or three magistrates; this meant that some sessions, for example at Gainsborough, might easily be dominated by Tories. The answer was to have fewer meetings attended by more magistrates, where Tories could be welcomed courteously, but kept in a minority. Under Brackenbury's re-organisation, after 1749 sessions met at only one town each quarter: Caistor at Epiphany (January); Spilsby at Easter; Gainsborough at Midsummer; and Louth at Michaelmas (October).

It seems likely that a system of petty sessions was also introduced in 1749. Magistrates were authorised to meet at certain times outside quarter sessions, to give judgement in matters requiring two justices and to deal with much routine local government business. Technically there were several different types of such meetings, but they were usually run together into what came to be called petty sessions. Practice varied, and early records are rare, so it is often very difficult to discover when the system was introduced in different parts of the country. Older authorities, like the Webbs, dated the emergence of petty sessions from the last quarter of the century. Recent research on marginal notes and details of sessions rolls has suggested an earlier date.[18]

The Lindsey evidence is far from conclusive, but a guess can be made. The sort of information the Webbs used confirms that there was a complete system of petty sessions in operation by the last quarter of the eighteenth century. In 1798 a large detailed map was produced to show the petty sessional divisions, giving the names of the magistrates, high constables and other officials who served each one.[19] We can be fairly certain that this machinery had been in place for some time. In 1792 Mr Dixon copied into his Justice Book:

> Notice - his majesty's justices of the peace in and near Louth intend to hold their meetings in the town hall of Louth every Wednesday fortnight throughout the year, from 11 a.m. to 2 p.m. The first meeting to be on 13 June 1792.[20]

The quarter sessions minutes confirm an extensive system in 1775, listing 'places where the Subdivision Meetings of the Justices are usually held', as Lincoln, Gainsborough, Caistor, Louth, Spilsby, Horncastle and Alford.[21]

Before 1775 the evidence is scanty, but there are a few chance references to petty sessions. The earliest is in 1754. On 23 June Bennet Langton received a complaint from Ivatts

Barton of Horncastle that George Dales had assaulted him in his own house, 'tearing the shirt off his back'. Langton 'gave a warrant to the Constable of Horncastle to apprehend and bring to Petty Sessions at Spilsby on Monday 20 July by 10 a.m. George Dales'.[22] Such slender clues are supported by the context of the re-organisation of 1749 and by certain changes in the types of offence which were tried at quarter sessions. Thus, it seems that petty sessions in Lindsey date from 1749.

7 THE COURTS AND CRIME 1750-70

a)   A More Formal System

Local justice did not disappear after 1749, but the courts became more formal, especially quarter sessions. Litigants now faced longer delays and journeys, and when they did reach the court they were confronted by an impressive array of magistrates: in the early days of the new system, as many as fifteen squeezed on to the bench. Even when common sense quickly reduced these numbers to half a dozen, the magistrates at sessions were drawn from a wider area and thus were less familiar.

Fewer defendants chose to traverse: whereas about fifteen chose to postpone and prepare their cases in this way each year in the 1740s, there was a sharp fall after 1749, and by the 1760s it was rare. This may have been because there was a longer wait before each sessions: this gave more time to prepare the case, and probably made the use of lawyers more routine. Certainly lawyers were being employed elsewhere, not in the modern sense of conducting the case, but it was increasingly the practice to allow them to stand beside the defendant, to advise him on what questions to ask and generally give counsel. It seems likely that this development did take place in Lindsey in mid-century, although the first explicit reference to the use of lawyers in criminal cases does not come until 1777.

At Midsummer sessions that year two labourers, William North and John Cole, were convicted of breaking into a warehouse at Coningsby and stealing eight stone of goose feathers. They were sentenced to imprisonment in the house of correction and to be publicly whipped. Such a case was fairly routine. Therefore the magistrates were surprised - there is a long entry in the minutes - at the next sessions when a Mr Calvert, 'solicitor for the prisoners', appeared. He reminded the court that his clients had been convicted on the evidence of a young accomplice. He pointed out, and even produced opinion from Counsel, that it was 'doctrine now universally received and allowed that the evidence of an accomplice unconfirmed is insufficient to convict'. Asserting his clients' innocence on these grounds, Mr Calvert went on to explain that their worships had created a rather difficult situation. As there was no error in the indictment, the only possibility was a pardon, which would take 'great time and expense'. He therefore suggested that his clients be released on bail 'to prevent the disagreeable consequence of a long imprisonment'. The magistrates may have been disconcerted, but they were not defeated. They said they would seek Counsel's advice. Next Epiphany sessions they appear to have convicted North and Cole of another theft and had them flogged for that.[1]

Apart from the introduction of more formal procedures, after 1749 there were significant changes in the types of case tried at quarter sessions. With only one meeting each quarter there was far more business to be dealt with and the clerk of the peace had to manage the load carefully, by sending many cases to other courts. As the records of these other courts have been lost it is impossible to quantify the change, but the pattern can be inferred from the sessions rolls.

More grand larceny cases appear to have been sent to assizes. In cases of theft, if goods were valued at more than one shilling, the offence was grand larceny, usually tried at assizes, and the convict might suffer death; if the goods were valued at less than one shilling the offence was petty larceny, tried at quarter sessions and punishable by flogging. In practice this distinction was less important by the eighteenth century because grand larceny was usually punished by transportation and this sentence could also be imposed at quarter sessions for petty larceny. Old traditions died hard, however, and most Lindsey indictments valued goods stolen at ten pence.

Probably the decision to undervalue goods in this way was largely in the hands of the prosecutor. In the 1740s it was quite common for serious thefts to be heard at sessions. In the decade 1740-9 twenty-two cases which were clearly grand larceny were tried at sessions and nine of those convicted were sentenced to transportation. After 1749 there is a marked change: in the two decades 1750-69 only five cases where valuations of goods indicate grand larceny were tried at sessions. No one was sentenced to transportation. The date, style and suddenness of this change surely indicate that the clerk of the peace was playing a more active role in valuations to manage the case-load at sessions.

At the other end of the scale, more petty business was also sent elsewhere. To all intents and purposes constables' presentments disappeared from sessions. They had been declining throughout the 1740s: in 1743 there had been eighty presentments by high and petty constables; in 1747 only twenty. After 1749, there were hardly any. The number of people prosecuted for keeping unlicensed ale-houses, that staple of the high constables' work, fell from 157 in 1740-9, to forty-three in 1750-9, and only seven in the 1760s.

There was a similar dramatic fall in a whole range of offences which had often been prosecuted by parish officers: the number of those refusing to pay rates or serve as parish officers fell from 111 in the 1740s to twenty-nine in 1750-9, and to just four in the 1760s. One hundred and sixty-seven vagrants were dealt with at sessions in 1740-9; in the 1750s the number fell to forty-four and rose to only fifty-four in 1760-9.

Quarter sessions virtually ceased to deal with those economic matters which had been such an important part of its work: 108 farming disputes had been heard in 1740-9; this fell to twenty-eight in the 1750s, with a further decline to twenty-four in the 1760s. In the 1740s there were still eighteen prosecutions for breach of the market laws; during the next twenty years there were only two; and whereas eleven disputes between masters and servants had been settled at sessions in the 1740s, no such cases were taken so far in the 1750s. Of course, such business did not cease; much of it was transferred to the new courts of petty sessions and some of the old relationships of 'vernacular justice' continued there.

The decline in administrative and economic business needs to be put in context - there was less business of all kinds in mid-century. The sessions bench dealt with about 1100 incidents in the 1740s; in the next two decades this number was halved to about 450 in the 1750s and to just over 500 in the 1760s. This cannot be accounted for by administrative changes and the transfer of business elsewhere. There was a real decline in the 'crime rate' at this time, part of a general trend which had begun in the late seventeenth century. The number of prosecutions for assault and theft was also halved, but the reduction here was far less than that in administrative and economic matters and there was a significant change in the types of cases tried at sessions. In the 1740s assaults made up about twenty per cent of all business but by the 1750s and 1760s this proportion rose to about thirty per cent. Thefts, which had formed only twelve per cent of all cases in the 1740s, rose to about sixteen per cent in the next two decades. All this amounted to an important shift in the character of quarter sessions. The court took much less responsibility for communal and economic regulation and became far more concerned with 'crime', with offences against the person and property. Private prosecutions increasingly replaced actions brought by parish officers on behalf of the community. The proceedings of the court were more formal, probably with more use of lawyers. Quarter sessions became more remote: the meetings were fewer and farther away; the justices were more intimidating because there were more of them and drawn from a wider area. No doubt Mr Brackenbury thought it was all more efficient and dignified and the magistrates preferred not to deal with so much of that petty business which had bored Stukely. It was good to have more gentlemen of all political views working together. The price was a greater distance between the gentry and the people; less 'vernacular justice' in the sense of responding to local needs; more concern with government and the control of crime.

b) Patterns of Crime

It should be emphasised that the 'crime rate', in reality a 'prosecution rate', of cases tried at sessions was very low. For the whole of Lindsey, (using the figures from the first accurate census of 1801) between 1740 and 1780 there were about twenty prosecutions for every 1,000 people: about one prosecution every two years for every thousand of the population.

Given this very low rate it is not possible to see intricate relationships between the figures and possible causes of crime. In broad terms the 'crime rate' fell in the 1740s, and remained low throughout the next two decades. The lowest point was reached at the end of the 1750s. Some, perhaps much, of this variation was due to administrative change, but other factors can be discovered. There was a relationship between hardship and theft, but it only showed up in the Lindsey figures in very difficult years. The terrible winter of 1741 produced over thirty prosecutions for theft, twice the normal figure. Harvest failure and food shortages in 1765 led to sixteen prosecutions, again about twice the usual figure at that time.

In London and other places in the country wars have been shown to affect crime. Assaults usually fall, possibly because many young men went away to fight. The war of the Austrian Succession ended in 1748, just when the Lindsey courts were re-organised, so no valid conclusions can be drawn. The Seven Years' War of 1757 to 1763 appears to have had little consistent effect on assaults, although the numbers did rise after the war: excluding exceptional cases, during the war there were about ten cases before the courts each year, as there had been throughout the 1750s. In the five years 1763-8 the average rose to fifteen.

Wars have also been shown to affect vagrancy, and the examinations in the Lindsey rolls contain many biographies of lives disrupted by wars and service in the armed forces. However, the statistics are not very convincing. The number of vagrants dealt with at quarter sessions fell very sharply after 1749: in most years there were only two or three cases. In three war years, 1757, 1760, and 1761, no vagrants were dealt with at sessions; but in 1762, towards the end of the war, the number jumped to twelve. However, only one of those vagrants claimed to have anything to do with the armed services: Mrs Lowry, arrested for wandering and begging in the Bail of Lincoln said she had been abandoned by her husband, who was 'now a soldier in the Scotch Fusiliers at Belleisle'.[2]

MAP 2
Distribution of Crime in Lindsey

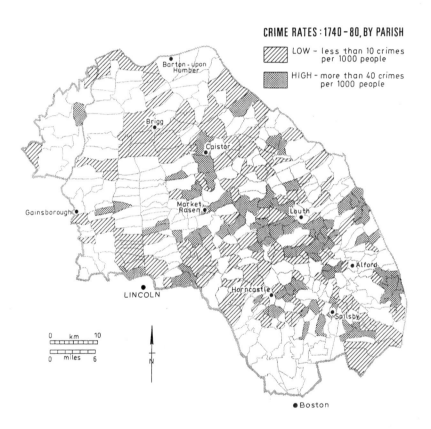

CRIME RATES : 1740 – 80, BY PARISH

LOW – less than 10 crimes per 1000 people

HIGH – more than 40 crimes per 1000 people

Barton - upon Humber

Brigg

Caistor

Market Rasen

Louth

Gainsborough

Alford

LINCOLN

Horncastle

Spilsby

0 km 10

0 miles 6

N

● Boston

In all these matters, the Lindsey numbers are so small that it is not possible to make real links between 'crime rates' and wars or minor fluctuations in the economic cycle. One of the most important factors in changing crime rates appears to have been administrative practice, particularly which court the clerk and the prosecutor decided to use. Without the records of assizes and petty sessions firmer conclusions are impossible.

An examination of the distribution of crime throughout the county produces more interesting results. Taking the raw figures the market towns suffered most crime, as might be expected. Gainsborough heads the list, with 159 prosecutions between 1740 and 1780. The other leaders were: Horncastle (74), Caistor (50), Barton (46), Market Rasen (39), Spilsby (38), Epworth (35), Kirton-in-Lindsey (33), Alford (30), Crowle (30) and Saltfleetby (20). At the other extreme, many small parishes have no crimes at all recorded in the sessions documents.

The raw figures become more revealing if they are related to population, to give 'crime rates' per head of residents. If this is done all but four of the market towns listed above turn out to have been no more criminal than the villages. Their rate was between thirty and thirty-five prosecutions per thousand people during the forty years and this was the average figure for all the larger villages.

Parishes can be arranged into three broad groups: those with average prosecution rates of between ten and forty cases per thousand inhabitants in the forty years 1740-80; those with exceptionally low rates of less than ten prosecutions per thousand; and those with exceptionally high rates of more than forty per thousand.

Most of the 'lows' are easily explained: many of them were small villages of less than one hundred people where informal control was probably strong. Others, larger settlements, were in the Ancholme valley, around Brigg, or east of Horncastle, where there were very few resident magistrates. Similarly, most of the 'highs' are simply accounted for: Caistor and Spilsby were busy market towns, but also sessions places; this made it easy for local people to prosecute, but it is also likely that some of the indictments are misleading, with the clerks hurriedly scribbling

'Caistor' or 'Spilsby' when the accused came from a nearby village. Other 'highs' like Harpswell and Stallingborough had active resident magistrates and may be explained in the same way.

Some of the 'highs' are much more mysterious; indeed, they are completely baffling. There was a large group of parishes to the west of Louth which consistently returned exceptionally high rates. These parishes stretch up the eastern slopes of the Wolds. They varied greatly in size, from South Reston (710 acres) to Tathwell (4326 acres). Their average population in 1801 was 143, but again there was wide variation, from Walmsgate, with fifty inhabitants, to Market Rasen with 774. Large or small, populous or sparsely settled, it made no difference; all these places had a higher crime rate than most similar parishes elsewhere.

It does not seem to be possible to explain this away by finding some quirk in the administration or records of the courts. These villages lay in several different wapentakes, different petty sessional divisions, even different quarter sessions divisions and were served by several different magistrates. Another possible answer might be proximity to Louth: the offences may have been committed in the busy town of Louth, but the residences of the accused were given on the indictments. This may certainly account for some of the extra offences recorded as having been committed in Caistor, Horncastle and Spilsby. However, it is a less satisfactory explanation for these Louth parishes. First, Louth had its own quarter sessions and dealt with its own crime; if anything, we should expect lower rates in the area. Second, there is no consistent pattern around the town: the parishes to the west have high rates, but those to the east are average or low.

Other possible explanations also fail: there does not seem to be any link with religion, patterns of enclosure or to any local character or event. Reluctantly, it seems necessary to accept that there is a genuine pattern here, that there was more crime, or people were more willing to prosecute, in these villages. It is very difficult to see why this should be the case. Most of these villages were nucleated settlements with standard parish organization. Perhaps the local farmers and landlords were disciplining and controlling workers more energetically in this fairly 'closed' environment. Perhaps there was an undercurrent of poaching, which does not show up in sessions records, but which meant farmers were more fearful and keener to prosecute other offences. Unfortunately, this sort of explanation will not stand. The increase in these parishes was not made up by crime against property and the extra prosecutions were not brought by employers.

Most of the high crime rate in these places is accounted for by more prosecutions for assault. In Lindsey as a whole between 1740 and 1780, assaults made up about twenty-three per cent of all crime; in these parishes thirty-seven per cent of crimes were assaults. As far as it is possible to tell from the indictments they were routine petty assaults, the prosecutor and victim being social equals. Although this seems to be a significant clue, it really does not take us very much further forward. How can it be explained? Could it be that life in a village of 150 people with unremitting work and little entertainment, became so oppressive that petty squabbles festered into violence and sessions cases? Surely such an answer is unsatisfactory; but that only leaves us with the possibility of some peculiarity in social or occupational structure or in the organization of petty sessions. At present the 'Louth highs' must be left unexplained.

8 THE TRANSFORMATION OF THE COUNTRYSIDE

a) The Landscape

The spirit of rational improvement which changed quarter sessions in the 1740s had much more dramatic effects when it was accompanied by the desire to make money. The 'revolutions' in transport and agriculture which took place in the eighteenth century are well-known and their impact on Lincolnshire has received thorough modern treatment elsewhere.[1] However, a brief summary is necessary here as background to the development of sessions in the 1770s. The most important points to make are that these economic changes reached a first crescendo in Lindsey in the middle years of the century, especially the 1760s, and that they really did transform the countryside.

Transport was greatly improved. Between 1739 and 1780 eight major turnpike trusts were founded in Lindsey and between them they took control of over 200 miles of road. This may be just the tip of the iceberg.[2] The sessions rolls show dozens of parishes levying new rates to improve their highways. On the other hand, a turnpike did not guarantee improvement. Arthur Young said Lincoln turnpikes were 'below par' and approaching Horncastle Viscount Torrington complained of 'a bad, hard road, tho' a turnpike'.[3] However, the scale and profit of the ventures, and the substantially increased traffic, were evidence of general improvement. Viscount Torrington was impressed by roads in the Louth and Spilsby areas, and declared the Spilsby to Boston turnpike to be 'of the greatest consequence'.[4]

The waterways were more spectacular. The old Roman canal from Lincoln to the Trent, the Fossdyke, had been restored to navigation and inspiring profitability after 1744.[5] There were major works on the Witham in the 1760s including large-scale drainage of the valley and control of the river for navigation, culminating in the building and famous opening of the Grand Sluice at Boston in 1766. The old Ancholme navigation was improved in 1767. Most impressive of all was the new canal linking Louth to the sea, making the town an inland port. Grundy and Smeaton's plan was approved by Act of Parliament in 1763 and work began in 1765. The first five miles were opened on 18 May 1767 and the whole cut was completed in May 1770. As with the turnpikes, these major undertakings were only the more visible peaks of much routine activity at a lower level. Drainage works went on throughout the county, especially in the Fens and Marshes. Six hundred and thirty acres were reclaimed in Tetney parish in 1778-9.[6]

Arthur Young, who complained about the huge wastes and barbarous practices which some farmers used when he first visited Lindsey in 1771, was struck by the progress which had been made when he came back in 1808. Then, he wrote: 'The most singular circumstance is, the very general improvement which has taken place ..., by the vast tracts which have been drained and cultivated.'[7] This surprise was partly because Young underestimated the Lindsey farmers on his first visit. They had been developing better agricultural techniques for many years. The Massingberds had been well-known for their innovations at the beginning of the century. Even in 1771 Young was impressed by the systematic experiments carried out by Sir Cecil Wray at Fillingham. New crops like sanfoin and turnips were common. The Norfolk four-course rotation was widely used as early as the 1750s and from about the same date the lands beside the Trent were being improved by warping.[8]

Above all there was enclosure. Many Lindsey parishes, especially those offering good pastures for grazing, had been enclosed in the sixteenth and seventeenth centuries. Piecemeal enclosure went forward quietly but steadily. However, few major schemes were undertaken in the early eighteenth century. There was little activity during the difficult years of 1720-50 with only five Lindsey enclosure Acts being passed during that time. The really dramatic change began in the 1760s, with seventy-five Acts being passed in twenty years.

These developments produced considerable economic and social progress. When the Fossdyke navigation was opened in 1744 the price of coal in Lincoln fell from twenty-one shillings to thirteen shillings a chaldron.[9] By the early nineteenth century Lincolnshire was sending 40,000 tons of grain each year to the textile towns of Lancashire and Yorkshire and in 1811 Boston exported one third of a million quarters of oats to London, which was a third of the capital's total consumption.[10] Fewer children died and the population began to increase. The death rate in the Marsh between 1760 and 1810 was half what it had been between 1676 and 1740 and on the Wolds it fell from thirty-four per thousand to twenty per thousand in the same periods.[11] Arthur Young pointed out the dramatic change at Winteringham. In the thirty years before enclosure births exceeded deaths by just fifty-nine; in the thirty years after by 209.[12]

Recent studies have revised the traditional picture of transport and agricultural 'revolutions' in the eighteenth century. Chambers and Mingay show that increases in production were slow at first and describe an 'Agricultural Revolution' stretching over two hundred years from 1660 to 1880. Dr Clark has wondered if there really was an industrial 'revolution' in the eighteenth century at all.[13] The Hammonds' view that enclosure was a 'violent catastrophe' which left 'disinherited peasants' sinking in the shadow of the wealth of unscrupulous landlords has not been confirmed by modern studies.[14] Work on Lindsey has shown that the enclosure commissioners acted fairly and the small farmers did not suffer. Dr Holderness goes so far as to say that he 'finds no example ... of a reduction in the numbers holding land being attributable, directly or indirectly, to the consequences of enclosure'.[15] Many of the smaller farmers had disappeared before, hit hard by the depression of the 1720s and 1730s.

All this may be true and the eighteenth-century changes may only have been part of slow and lengthy developments taking place over two hundred years or more, but there is still a strong case for saying that it was in the 1760s and 1770s that these changes first struck home. To the ordinary people of Lindsey, the late 1760s and the 1770s must have appeared to be a time of rapid and bewildering change, because it was then that the subtle effects of deep economic forces became visible as they transformed the landscape.

Eye-witness accounts by visitors to the county constantly refer to the new drains, fences, hedges, and roads. Thomas Quincey, who toured Lindsey in 1772, was greatly impressed by the sense of prosperity and rapid progress:

> I must beg leave to digress a moment, in order to call the reader's attention to the many public-spirited undertakings of this county. Indeed, the innumerable drains, rivers, artificial banks, sluices, bridges, engines, etc., together with the strict attention that has been paid in the first instance to the preservation of these works, and the keeping of them in order, all these, with the number and excellence of the turnpike roads, conspire to raise in the traveller a very lofty idea of the opulence and industry of the inhabitants.[16]

The changes which we have to infer from statistics were obvious to him. The towns were thriving. Of Boston, he wrote: 'Boston, upon the whole, though not a very large town, is a thriving place. ... Its trade of sending oats to London is so much upon the increase, that several large granaries are now erecting purposely for that article.'[17] He found similar signs of activity at Lincoln. Visitors before 1760 had usually noticed only Gothic architecture and decay. What Quincey saw was 'the considerable trade carried on', and, stacked beside the Fossdyke, 'the greatest quantity of fine ship timber that I ever saw in one place, probably brought down the Trent or some of the rivers of the West Riding of Yorkshire'.[18]

Louth had an even greater impact on John Cragg in 1799. As soon as he had put up at the Blue Stone inn he walked down to see the canal. He found the basin 'spacious', capable of taking vessels up to fifty tons, and very active: 'There seems to be a deal of business done at it in coal, corn, and wool carriage.' He saw 'a vessel building', and several warehouses for wool and granaries for wheat ... built by the canal-side, which looks like a town at a distance'. He also inspected 'a woollen manufactory, with about twenty machines in two buildings , which carded, spun, and reeled the wool, almost all turned by water ... very curious'. He completed his evening tour with a visit to the new carpet factory, where he saw 'several looms employed in weaving those curious pieces of furniture'. On reflection, he recognised the considerable benefits these places created in 'the employment of children and persons to manage them', but thought the town suffered from 'the smell of the oil and the wool ... very unpleasant'.[19]

However, it was in the rural areas that the changes were most spectacular as drainage and enclosure swept away traditional landscapes. Hundreds of miles of new, straight, forty-foot roads were laid out. Everywhere there were new, straight-edged fields, bounded by fresh rails or hawthorn hedges. What had previously been fen and moor became vast seas of oats or barley. All the travellers comment on these changes. Torrington, in the summer of 1791, refers again and again to 'a country now drain'd and enclosed' (Witham); 'all enclosed and flourishing with corn' (Swineshead); 'new enclosures'(Moreby). The Wolds near Barton were 'lately enclosed' and south of Lincoln was 'all newly-enclosed heath'. As he left the county he concluded, 'the Fens, once a scene of wretchedness, are now the gayest part, and the best inhabited'.[20]

The cultivation of the wastes and Fens impressed Arthur Young when he returned to Lindsey in 1808. Compared with his first visit over thirty years before, 'Upon the whole ... perhaps the most singular circumstance is, the very general improvement which has taken place ... by the vast tracts which have been drained and cultivated, a work which is still going on'.[21] The Wolds from Spilsby to Caistor, 'all warren for thirty miles' in 1771, had been made 'by turnips and seed' into land which supported 'twenty sheep where there had been one before'.[22] But even in the early seventies much work had already been done in the Fens. Approaching Lincoln from the Witham valley in 1772, Quincey remarked: 'The Fens I have just mentioned, used to present a disgusting view of mud, weeds, etc., but are lately enclosed, intersected by white thorn hedges, and now appear in one continued field of oats.'[23] On his way to Boston, he saw 'this extensive heath ... lately enclosed', bearing 'excellent crops, of barley in particular'.[24]

As Dr Thirsk has written, all this was 'a real revolution which transformed the landscape'.[25] Even the least-travelled inhabitant of the remotest village in Lindsey must have seen what was happening. Modern historians may discern that these changes were gradual and had been long in the making; for ordinary people they became suddenly and spectacularly visible in the late 1760s and 1770s.

b) A People's Revolt?
Even if the revolutions in agriculture and transport were beneficial in the long run, at the time they caused great disruption of traditional life and work, disturbing patterns which had existed for centuries. Often too, in the early years, they seemed to be for the benefit of the richer farmers, landowners and merchants at the expense of those who used the commons and the Fens. And in the 1770s all this was not something theoretical, a current beneath the surface. It was all suddenly there, concrete, throughout all the villages: new fences, new roads, ditches, and hedges; the old pathways blocked up, the commons removed. How did the ordinary people react to this? Did they accept, or rise in protest?

The first point to make is that riot and disorder were commonplace. The eighteenth century would have laughed at the fuss late twentieth-century Britain makes about its minor disorders. Even in the countryside assaults were the most common crimes, and the sessions rolls show there was already a good deal of juvenile violence. Youths 'assembled in a riotous and unlawful manner' to pull up householders' gates and fences.[26] They threw stones at the windows of prosperous shopkeepers and citizens.[27] They harassed people they did not like: one old lady told magistrates that the young men of Fiskerton had 'put her in bodily fear' by 'riotously assembling and ... threatening to duck her'.[28] They scrumped and turned nasty if they were caught: John Pell of Binbrook prosecuted some young men for 'unlawfully entering into his orchard and beating down the apples and breaking his orchard gate and threatening to pull down his dwelling house and behaving in a riotous manner'.[29]

Innkeepers suffered often with drunken mobs around their houses late at night, breaking windows and doors over some real or imagined grievance.[30] Clergymen were also targets. The minister at Waltham was 'molested and disturbed in the publick and Divine Service' by Hannah Resdale who made 'several scandalous and infamous declamations'.[31] He was luckier than the rector of Withern, who had a mob around his house one night 'for one-and-a-quarter hours' in 1772.[32] The trials of John Wesley are well-known, although they only led to one action at sessions in Lindsey. The constable of Epworth testified:

> On Saturday the 6 July 1776 between the hours of 7 and 8 p.m. he was in company with a great many people in a Society house in Epworth to hear one John Wesley, Minister of the gospel of the Church of England preach, ... and during that time one Benjamin Barton of Epworth, saddler, behaved in a very riotous manner, and that he, as Constable of Epworth, was desired to take care of him, and went to charge him with the King's Peace, ... and the said Benjamin Barton immediately struck him with a large stick over his head.[33]

Often there was real venom and bitterness in these disturbances, such as would have terrified the ruling classes of early nineteenth-century England. In 1767 there was a strike among the cordwainers and shoemakers of Brigg 'to raise their wages'. When the men in William Lawson's shop continued working some of the strikers came 'riotously' to 'demand the tools belonging to the workmen ... with intent to prevent them working' and when Lawson tried to stop them they threatened 'to knock out his eyes'.[34]

Arson threats were reported on several occasions. The trustees of Goxhill workhouse were verbally abused by the local schoolmaster who told them 'he would turn out all the people in the workhouse on Monday and then he would set it on fire'.[35] Robert Newton of Stallingborough threatened a farmer that he would 'burn his haystack' if he was prosecuted for theft.[36] Sarah and Susannah Taylor 'threatened to burn the poor houses in Alford, and the House of Correction'.[37]

Further, this was a society which had seen major disturbances. There had, after all, been a real civil war in 1745. The militia riots of 1756-7 had been events of national importance and were particularly severe in Lindsey. Such a background lent added significance to minor events. In 1774, when the list of men liable to serve in the militia was fixed to the church door in Spilsby it was torn down by John Harrison, a cordwainer.[38] So this was a society which knew real instability and suffered from endemic violence and disorder, some of it vicious and threatening. The people knew how to riot. How did they respond to enclosure?

In the Fens there was revolt. As part of the Witham improvement scheme an Act to enclose Holland Fen, 'the Haute Huntre', was obtained in 1767. Next summer, as the work began, the people rose against the scheme. In July 1768, the *Stamford Mercury* reported:

> On Thursday last there was 1000 persons assembled at Donington, most of them armed with firearms and scythes, straightened and fixed in shafts, expecting to meet a body of men from Boston-side of whom they had information. ... A gentleman of Boston went among them and expostulated with them of the unlawfulness of such associations, but without effect, for they declared that they would not injure any person, but that the fen should not be enclosed, nor their common rights taken away from them, which they would support and defend with the utmost hazard of their lives. [39]

They meant what they said. Although the deployment of the Scots Greys prevented the firing of Boston, they could not stop the new fences being pulled down as soon as they were erected. This really was what a modern historian of Boston calls 'an insurrection'. For five years the area was gripped by 'a sickening succession of murder and attempted murder, of maiming people and animals, of incendiarism and other barbarities'. One man 'was shot dead as he sat by his fireside', and

> Mr Garfit, a Boston merchant, and Robert Barlow had coach horses poisoned, and Mrs Barlow was shot in the head as she sat by her fire: her husband had just left the room 'otherwise from the direction in which the ball came he must have been killed in his chair'. Other houses were fired, and barns and stacks were also set ablaze. Mr J. Tunnard had about fifty fine sheep hamstrung, Herbert Ingram had 'a horse shot worth twenty pounds', and Robert Creasey ... had 'some ewes and lambs barbarously killed by having their backs broken'.[40]

In the Fens such violence might be expected. In the seventeenth century the great-grandfathers of these rioters had also resisted the 'improvers'. Would they now provide an example to others? In the rest of Lindsey the first spasm of enclosure of the open fields was just reaching a peak at the time of the fen riots, with 127 enclosure Acts between 1760 and 1780. Would these new fences also be torn down, the farmers and commissioners resisted?

The sessions rolls contain little evidence of any violent reaction. There were some trivial incidents. During the enclosure of Ingham in 1770 a labourer stole some of the new fence rails, but apparently it was for firewood, rather than a protest.[41] At Winterton, also enclosed in 1770, there seems to have been some trouble as the new fences went up. In June 1774 two young men were fined one shilling each 'for breaking rails and grass by walking on the new allotments of land called the Cliffs'.[42] A case at Keelby, enclosed in 1765, appears to have been more serious. There, in December 1772, Francis

Atkinson 'on several days did enter certain new enclosed allotment land called the Five Acres ... and did damage and destroy turnips growing there, and break, disturb and destroy the banks, quicks, rails, and fences'.[43] He was fined sixpence. There was an exactly similar case at Middle Rasen (enclosed 1772-4) in 1775, when two young men were each fined ten shillings for 'entering into the new inclosed allotment called Scatter-wit, and damaging the grass by walking, and breaking the banks and quick hedges'.[44] Possibly the most serious event occurred at Tetney. Just as proceedings for enclosure were beginning in November 1775, some young men were fined ten shillings 'for riotously assembling in the night time', threatening a farmer, and breaking his waggon.[45]

But that is all. There is no evidence of any general change in the 'crime rate' of parishes before and after enclosure. Most of the handful of cases, with the possible exception of Tetney, seem to have been nothing more than people pushing through the new hedges to follow the ancient footpaths, used for generations but now stopped up. The small fines imposed suggest that there was no great concern by landowners and farmers. In short, there is no evidence of any serious protest at the enclosure of the open fields in Lindsey.

Perhaps enclosure was more familiar to local people than the travellers thought: many parishes here had been enclosed in the sixteenth and seventeenth centuries; many of the remaining open-field villages had large areas of old enclosures; the process of parliamentary enclosure was slow, often taking years to complete. But on the other hand all the visitors to the county agree on the visual impact of the new fences, hedges, roads, and closes. The fen rioters gave example at precisely the right moment and those new boundaries were tender and easy targets for attack. Could it be that the people simply accepted enclosure, recognised that it was an improvement?

One thing is clear: it was the change in attitude created by the French Revolution rather than simple economic change which marked the real turning-point. After 1789 there would be no more sixpenny fines for breaking fences, and those riotous assemblies of young men, those quickly-hurled threats, would take on an altogether different significance. In 1830, those young men from Tetney would have been transported or hanged. As yet, the gentry accepted a high level of violence as inevitable and customary; they were confident that their improvements really were rational improvements; and, for the most part, they seem to have carried the people with them. Without that confidence and stability the process of economic change might have been very different.

9 THE 1770s - A NEW SYSTEM OF GOVERNMENT

There is a striking change in the sessions documents from the late sixties onwards. The rolls become thicker and better organised, the minutes are longer, and full of new regulations and procedures. Much more business came before the bench. In the 1750s and 1760s they had dealt with about 500 cases each decade. In the 1770s the workload increased by half to 765. Probably this was simply due to increased population, although the magistrates could not know this at the time. Of course they were aware of the extra business and as early as 1766 the Spilsby bench protested that there was too much to deal with in one sitting each quarter. After much discussion with the other divisions and advice from Counsel a new system was adopted in 1769. Henceforward there were to be two sittings each quarter, one in the eastern division of the county, one in the west. Thus sessions might originate at Gainsborough and adjourn to Louth, or begin at Spilsby and adjourn to Caistor. No doubt this created a momentum of its own: more convenient courts encouraged more litigants.

These changes were accompanied by a thorough overhaul of administration. The improvements were carried out by a new clerk of the peace, Robert Chapman, appointed in 1771. The rules governing the attendance of chief constables, petty constables and bailiffs at sessions were rationalised, printed, and enforced. Three chief constables were fined for non-attendance to drive the message home.[1] At Michaelmas 1771 the new clerk was ordered to 'enter into a book the chief constables' fees, and make a table thereof' so that they might be published throughout the county.[2] In 1772 it was ordered 'that twenty-four wands be provided for the constables and bailiffs at each sessions and locked up in some convenient places in Louth and Spilsby' for the better ceremonial performance of their duties at sessions.[3] New sets of legal books were ordered for each of the sessions towns: Pruffhead's *Statutes*, Burrows' *Settlement Cases*, Ward and Cunningham's *Justice*, Burn's *Justice*. Together with the *Statutes of the Realm*, they were to be embossed and kept in locked cases.[4] The whole process culminated in the decision to publish a printed booklet of 'The Rules and Orders Concerning the Practice of the Court of General Quarter Sessions of the Peace for the Parts of Lindsey' so that the new procedures might be formalised and understood by all.

There was a new passion for lists and accurate records. Often these were required by the central government by new Act of Parliament, but others were requested by the local magistrates and officials who wanted to investigate present policy and improve it. In 1775 it was ordered that 'The Treasurer give account of the money spent on vagrants, on the apprehension and passage of persons confined in the House of Correction in 1772, 1773, and 1774.' The bench also wanted 'Accounts from the Keepers of the Houses of Correction of how long vagrants ... were kept in the Houses of Correction, and that the median thereof be taken for a year'.[5] In 1776, in response to a House of Commons order, returns were made 'of all persons transported since 1 November 1769'.[6] The largest task was undertaken in 1776. All chief constables were ordered to attend sessions to receive instructions on 'requiring the overseers of the poor in every parish to make returns to certain questions regarding the state of the poor'; and, in keeping with the more efficient bureaucracy 'they received printed copies of the schedule, to be delivered to all Overseers of the Poor'.[7]

All this was moving beyond mere rationalisation and efficiency. Sessions was becoming part of a national system of government. Many of the magistrates did want to govern: they were no longer content, like Stukely, just to turn up and deal with whatever business the locals brought before them. They wanted to play a more active role: to govern, improve, reform. They even tried to catch more criminals. Some of this came from London, where there had been more concern about crime since the 1750s. It came to Lindsey in the form of letters from the famous London magistrate, Sir John Fielding. He regularly addressed suggestions for improvement to the county benches. His first recorded contact with Lindsey was in 1772 when he circulated 'a list and descriptions' of certain wanted men. The response was enthusiastic: the justices ordered that the list 'be reprinted and distributed to the Chief Constables and to be by them sent to all Petty Constables, and to be stuck up on the Church door of each parish ... and the expenses to be paid by the County Treasurer'.[8]

In 1773 a further request from Fielding for a national system of information about criminals prompted the magistrates to order 'that the Keepers of the House of Correction ... start books giving the name, age, nativity, height, trade, short description, place of abode, and committing magistrate of their prisoners'. The clerk was to insist that the county gaoler make similar lists for his prison. Further, the clerk was to write to Sir John, explaining how the justices were using and adapting his system of recording offenders 'and to thank him for his zeal and attention to the public service, and to desire him to send his weekly papers'.[9]

However, there were limits. When Fielding proposed a system of appointing more constables to watch the main roads for wanted men the Lindsey magistrates replied

> that they very much approved of the plan, ... But that the Division of Lindsey does not adjoin upon any of the four great roads mentioned in Sir John's letter, and is situated upwards of one hundred miles from London, that few offenders escaping from London come into these Parts, and therefore the Justices do not think it necessary to appoint an additional number of Petty Constables within this Division.

However, in a revealing demonstration of their enthusiasm for Sir John's schemes they promised

> to give it in charge to the Chief Constables and Petty Constables within this Division to be very vigilant in the execution of their office, and have ordered Lists of the Names and Places of Abode of the Chief Constables within this Division to be transmitted to the Office in Bow Street.[10]

This more positive, active policy was also extended to the control of vagrants. In 1766 the bench received from the lord lieutenant an Order of the Privy Council 'recommending in the strongest terms ... that the laws against Rogues and Vagabonds and other idle and disorderly persons' be carried into 'the strictest execution'. Again, this met a ready response from the bench. They ordered that

> Warrants should be forthwith issued to the Chief Constables and Petty Constables ... to search for and apprehend immediately and from Time to Time, all Rogues, Vagabonds, loose, idle, and disorderly persons as shall be found in any place within their Divisions, and forthwith carry the persons so apprehended before some of His Majesty's Justices of the Peace.[11]

From such measures it was not far to the improvement of manners or at least, to attempts to assist the personal salvation of the poor. At the same sessions which ordered the stricter pursuit of vagrants they made the following order concerning a law of 1677, 'An Act for the better Observation of the Lord's Day':

> It is enacted that all laws in force concerning the Observation of the Lord's Day and repairing to Church thereon be carefully put into execution, and that all Persons shall on every Lord's Day apply themselves to Observation of the same, by

exercising themselves thereon in Piety and true religion, publicly and privately, and that no tradesman or artificer, Labourer or other Person shall do any worldly work or Labour of their ordinary calling upon the Lord's Day ... And that any Person over the Age of 14 offending shall be fined five shillings.

No Person shall cry or expose for Sale any goods, or they shall forfeit the same goods.

No Drover, Horse Courser, Waggoner, Butcher, or Higgler shall travel or come into their Inns upon the Lord's Day; fine twenty shillings.

No travel with any Boat, Lighter, or Barge except upon any extraordinary occasion to be allowed by a Justice of the Peace; fine five shillings.

It is ordered by this Court, and by the Justices of the Peace here Present, that any Innkeeper or Alehousekeeper suffering therein any Tippling or other offences mentioned above shall be prosecuted; and it is also ordered that all Churchwardens, Overseers of the Poor, Chief Constables, Petty Constables, and all other peace officers within the said Parts be very vigilant and strict in the Discovery and effectual Prosecution of such who shall be guilty of any of the offences aforesaid, which the said Justices do hereby declare their purpose and resolution to punish to the utmost Rigour.

It is ordered that the Clerk do get Copies of this order printed and sent to the Chief Constables, Petty Constables, and Churchwardens of each Parish within this Sub-Division of the said Parts, and that copies thereof be fixed upon each Church Door and in the most publick Places in each

Market Town and village within the said
Sub-Division.[12]

Apparently they meant it. In November 1776 three
Gainsborough men were prosecuted 'for hauling a ketch upriver
on a Sunday'.[13]

All this was quite new: the magistrates were adopting a more
active, interventionist, reforming, approach and they were using
the ancient local government officers to carry out policies
imposed from above. It was a much more ambitious approach
to government; they were trying to change the people. Earlier in
the eighteenth century this would not have seemed possible.
Many gentlemen had regarded the poor as too ignorant, too
unreasonable, to be improved; they had simply been controlled
by flogging or by a justice resolving their silly squabbles. The
new attitude was not limited to reformation of manners, to
greater vigilance in finding criminals and vagrants, or enforcing
Sunday observance. There was also a new humanitarianism. By
the 1770s a growing number of people simply could not tolerate
the harsh treatment suffered by many of their fellow human
beings and there was a new concern for the poor, the weak, and
the oppressed.

The early results of this humanitarianism are well-known:
Jonas Hanway's work for pauper apprentices; Captain Coram's
Foundling Hospital; Raikes' Sunday Schools; the anti-slavery
movement. The mood had already penetrated Lindsey. At the
assizes in 1768 the grand jury took up a proposal for 'an hospital
for the sick and lame poor of this county' and in 1769 the
hospital was established in a house in Lincoln, with 'room for
ten in-patients and forty out-patients'. By 1777 the house had
been replaced by a purpose-built hospital of twenty-four beds
designed by John Carr.[14]

Within the penal system, humanitarianism meant better
treatment for prisoners. John Howard was in Lindsey in 1774
and 1776, and condemned Lincoln gaol: the dungeons were
'offensive' and there was no water, no sewer, no chapel, no
infirmary.[15] However, the Lindsey justices were already taking
steps to improve the houses of correction. In 1773 the quarter
sessions grand jury at Louth had presented the house of

correction 'as not sufficient, and wants to be enlarged'.[16] Their example was immediately followed by the grand jury at Gainsborough, who presented their house as 'unhealthy on account of the dampness of the floor of the four Prison rooms, and that the out door near the yard and the window of the working shop are insufficient'. Committees of justices were established to 'contract with workmen' to make improvements.[17]

In October 1773 the bench took into consideration 'the Act for providing clergymen for gaols' and appointed one to the county gaol, but resolved 'that it is not necessary that any clergyman be appointed to the ... Houses of Correction... on account of the small number of prisoners usually confin'd there'.[18] Real improvement came in 1774 when the court read the Act of Parliament for 'Preserving the Health of Prisoners and Preventing Gaol Distemper'. The justices ordered that

> the walls, seilings (sic) of cells and Wards of debtors and felons and any other rooms used by prisoners in the Castle of Lincoln and the House of Correction at Gainsborough be scraped and whitewashed once in the year at least, to be regularly washed and kept clean and constantly supplied with fresh air, and two rooms in the Castle of Lincoln, one for men and the other for women, to be set apart for sick Prisoners, and that they be removed into such Rooms as soon as they shall be seized with any Disorder and kept separate from those who shall be in health.

> And that a Bathing Tub be made and kept for the use of the Prisoners, to be used as a Warm Bath, and that this Act be painted in large and legible Characters upon a Board, and hung up in some conspicuous part of the said Gaol and House of Correction at Gainsborough.

> And that Mr Paul Pannell be appointed Surgeon and Apothecary at a Salary of £10 per annum, ... and to report to the Justices ... at each Quarter Sessions on the State of Health of the Prisoners under his care or Supervision.[19]

The 1770s also saw considerable changes in the composition of the bench. More active magistrates had to be appointed to cope with the increased work. In the decade 1740-9 there had been thirty-one active magistrates; during the next two decades, about twenty-five; in the ten years 1770-9 the number jumped to forty-one. This was a visible and striking change: eight new justices were sworn in at a single sessions in 1771.[20]

Some of the new justices of the peace were men of a different type. In the 1740s about a quarter of the magistrates had come from 'old' families, families established in their areas since the middle of the seventeenth century. Their grandfathers had judged the grandfathers of those who came before them. By the 1770s only about fifteen percent of active magistrates came from such families. Also, the number of clerics on the bench increased slightly from thirteen to fifteen per cent. The change was expressed by two personalities. Old Thomas Whichcot made his last appearance at quarter sessions in 1774. At Michaelmas that year a man of the new type took his place on the bench. He was a clergyman, the Reverend Reynold Gideon Bouyer. His pluralism, for he was rector of Theddlethorpe and vicar of Willoughby, marked him as a man of the eighteenth century, but in other ways he was a herald of the Victorian age. He attended sessions regularly and supported the new reforming measures whole-heartedly and he was also active in promoting philanthropic work. He began the 'Society for the Promotion of Industry' in 1783, which was a scheme to employ the poor in making stockings, carpets, and blankets. He tried to establish spinning schools in rural areas. These were to be subsidised by the poor rates and the children were to be 'taught to card and spin coarse wool', and 'kept in good order'. Later, he went on to found public libraries in Northumberland.[21]

New magistrates, humanitarianism, reforming zeal and the revolutionary economic changes, produced a different pattern of crime in the 1770s. Economic regulation was virtually abandoned. The last spasm of attempts to enforce the laws of the market had been during the famine years of 1765-6. In the 1770s only seven offences against these laws were prosecuted at sessions, and they were only cases of false weights and measures. In the 1740s, 106 petty disputes between farmers had been settled at sessions; in the 1770s there were only eighteen. Only two quarrels between masters and servants were heard. In all, whereas regulation of the market, the open fields, and masters and servants had formed twelve per cent of all business in the 1740s, by the 1770s it was only three per cent. Probably this reflected real change: enclosed fields and growing acceptance of individualistic economics needed less regulation.

The number of assaults tried at sessions declined sharply in the 1770s, down to less than a quarter of all business. The reduction was even more marked if we consider assaults as a proportion of all 'crimes' which came before the courts, ignoring administrative business, like unlicensed ale-houses. Assault had always been the largest category of 'criminal' business, making up just over half of it during 1740 to 1770. In the 1770s it dropped to one third. Perhaps this was because enclosed villages were less violent or more strictly controlled by employers; more likely, it was because these trivial fights were now being settled at petty sessions. They were no longer important enough for quarter sessions. The transfer of cases to petty sessions accounts for the fall in all business heard at quarter sessions at the end of the seventies. It was a vain attempt to reduce the workload: in the 1780s and 1790s the inexorable upward trend resumed.

The matters which were thought important enough to be dealt with at sessions in the 1770s reveal an interesting pattern. Prosecutions for disorder, minor disturbances involving small groups of people, doubled. In the 1740s there had been twenty-four such cases but in the 1770s, fifty-four - an increase from two to seven per cent of all business. More poaching cases were heard. Above all, there was an increase in the number of thefts tried at sessions. The figure rose to 170 in the 1770s, higher than it had ever been in the period. Thefts now made up twenty-two per cent of all cases as opposed to twelve per cent in the 1740s.

Even more striking, offences against property overtook assaults as the largest category of prosecutions in the 1770s, forming just over a quarter of all business. The sentence of transportation returned to sessions. During the years of careful management of caseload, 1750-70, cases likely to require transportation had been reserved for assizes. Between 1770 and 1780 the quarter sessions bench sentenced ten people to be transported.

By the 1770s quarter sessions had changed to reflect new conditions and the different concerns and anxieties of the governing classes. The bench took a more active role in governing the people and they were becoming more concerned with 'real crimes', especially offences against property, than with settling trivial disputes. 'Vernacular justice' had been replaced by a system of government from above.

Yet it would be wrong to give the impression that the magistrates were afraid, struggling to control rapid economic and social change. Setting out on his tour into Lincolnshire in 1791, Viscount Torrington wrote:

> If my journals should remain legible, or be perused at the end of two hundred years, there will, even then, be little curious in them relative to travel, or the people; because our island is now so explored; or roads, in general, are so fine, and our speed has reach'd its summit.[22]

This curious comment may be taken to sum up the attitude of many of the old Lindsey justices. They were proud of their achievement. Their hard work, their 'reason', had helped to create the stability and economic improvements of mid-century. But their common sense was stronger than their imagination. Their sense of history was rather static, locked into classical times. It was a good model for patricians, but it limited their ability to imagine the future. They were confident that their rational improvements were just improvements and they had little conception of the forces they had helped to unleash.

TABLE 2
Numbers of Incidents before Lindsey Quarter Sessions 1740–80

Incident	1740-9	1750-9	1760-9	1770-9	Total
Assault	228	124	148	183	683
Theft	132	74	74	170	450
Vagrancy	167	46	54	71	338
Bastardy	81	48	61	119	309
Ale-house	206	33	7	9	255
No Duties	111	29	4	50	194
Farming	106	28	24	18	176
Disorder	23	24	32	54	133
Poaching	23	9	5	16	53
Profane Oath	6	7	24	11	48
Fraud	16	5	9	15	45
Market	18	1	1	7	27
Poor Law	7	1	8	10	26
Sex Offences	6	3	14	1	24
Master/Servt	11	0	7	2	20
Receiving	2	2	3	9	16
Misc.	18	13	30	20	81
Totals	**1161**	**447**	**505**	**765**	**2878**
Summary	**19**	**12**	**27**	**26**	**82**

Ale-house = Selling ale without licence.
No Duties = Refusal to serve as parish officer or pay rates
Disorder = Disturbances involving more than two people.
Bastardy = Number of bastardy bonds enroled.
Sex Offences includes keeping brothels.
Summary = Number of summary convictions enroled.

TABLE 3
Percentages of Incidents at Lindsey Quarter Sessions 1740-80

Incident	1740-9	1750-9	1760-9	1770-9	Total
Assault	20.5	28.0	29.0	24.0	24.0
Disorder	2.0	5.5	6.5	7.0	4.5
Sex Offences	0.5	0.5	3.0	0	1.0
Profane Oath	0.5	1.5	5.0	1.5	1.5
Theft	12.0	16.5	14.5	22.0	16.0
Receiving	0	0.5	1.0	1.0	0.5
Fraud	1.5	1.0	2.0	2.0	1.5
Market	1.5	0	0	1.0	1.0
Farming	9.5	6.5	5.0	2.5	6.0
Master/Servt	1.0	0	1.5	0.5	0.5
No Duties	10.0	6.5	1.0	6.5	7.0
Ale-house	18.5	7.5	1.5	1.0	7.5
Poor Law	0.5	0	1.5	1.5	1.0
Poaching	2.0	2.0	1.0	2.0	2.0
Vagrancy	15.0	10.0	10.5	9.0	12.0
Bastardy	7.5	11.0	12.0	15.5	11.0
Misc.	1.5	3.0	5.5	3.5	3.0

TABLE 4
All Events
(Annual Totals)

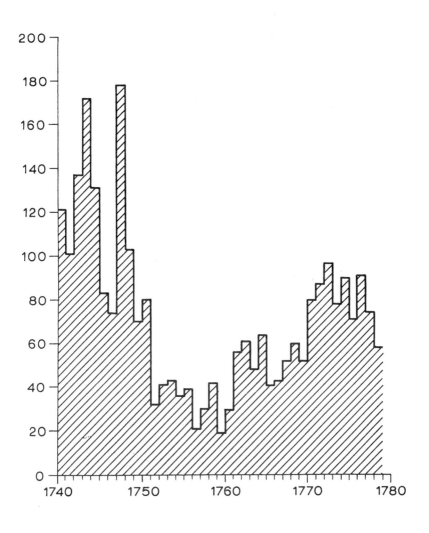

TABLE 5
Assaults
(Triennial Totals)

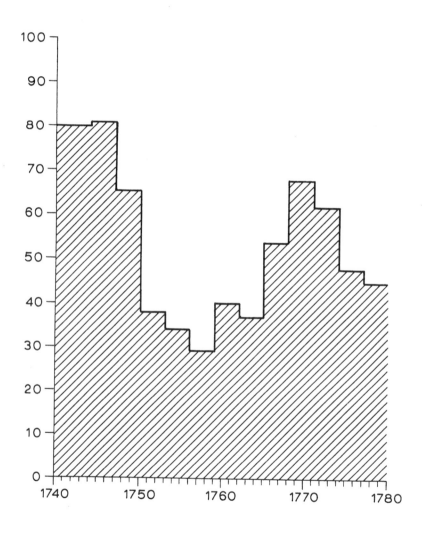

TABLE 6
Thefts
(Triennial Totals)

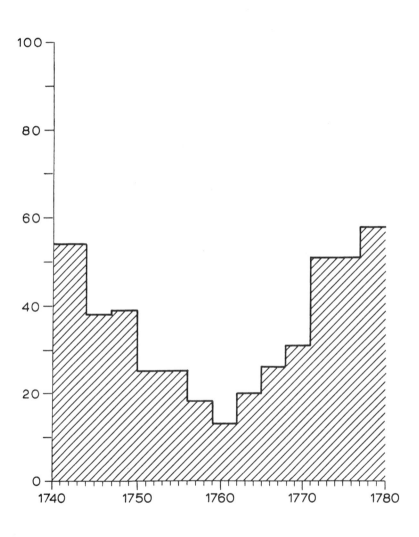

TABLE 7
Bastardy Bonds
(Triennial Totals)

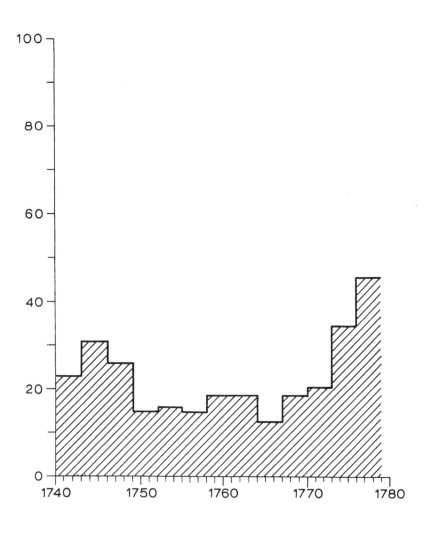

TABLE 8
Vagrancy
(Triennial Totals)

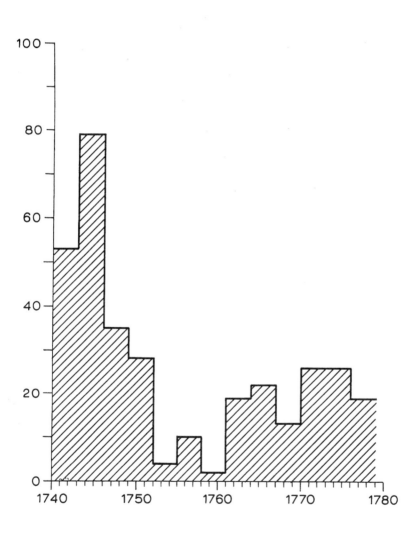

TABLE 9
Disorder
(Triennial Totals)

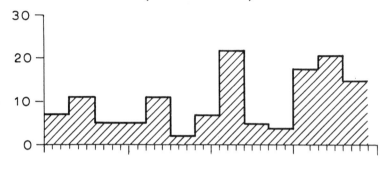

TABLE 10
Poaching
(Triennial Totals)

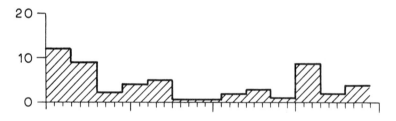

TABLE 11
Farming
(Triennial Totals)

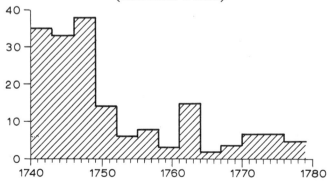

NOTES

Notes to Introduction

1.   T. Quincey, 'Tour of the Midland Counties of England, Summer 1772', *Gentleman's Magazine* LXIV (1774) 253.
2.   A. de la Pryme, *The Diary of Abraham de la Pryme*, ed. C. Jackson (Surtees Society, LIV, 1864) 58-9.
3.   D. Defoe, *A Tour Through the Whole Island of Great Britain* (London, 1724-6) 2, 95.
4.   T.W. Beastall, *The Agricultural Revolution in Lincolnshire* (Lincoln, 1979) 46.
5.   B.A. Holderness, 'Rural Society in South-East Lindsey, 1660-1840' (University of Nottingham Ph.D., 1968) 263.
6.   Ibid., 395.
7.   Sir Francis Hill, *Georgian Lincoln* (Cambridge, 1966) 51.
8.   Ibid., 259.
9.   LAO, Tennyson, 2/1/24.
10.   S.A. Peyton (ed.), *Minutes of Proceedings in Quarter Sessions held for the Parts of Kesteven in the County of Lincoln 1674-1695* (LRS 25, Lincoln, 1931) I, xiii-cxliv.

Notes to Chapter 1

1.   G.M. Trevelyan, *Illustrated English Social History* (London, 1942) 3, 47.
2.   J.A. Sharpe, *Crime in Early Modern England 1550-1750* (London, 1984) 58-64.
3.   Defoe, *Tour*, 2, 94.
4.   Hill, *Georgian Lincoln* 26.
5.   C.M. Lloyd (ed.), *Letters from John Wallace to Madam Whichcot* (LRS 66, Lincoln, 1973), 19.
6.   Ibid., 20-1.
7.   E. Peacock, 'The Rebellion of 1745', *LNQ* no.1 (1888-9) 67.
8.   Hill, *Georgian Lincoln* 84-5.
9.   *LRSM* 9 Jan. 1746.
10.   G.G. Walker and W.A. Cragg, 'Proceedings on Account of the Rebellion in 1745', *LNQ* no. 12 (1912-13) 238-41.
11.   A77 Mc 1746.
12.   Anon., *The Date Book for Lincoln and Neighbourhood* (R.E. Leary, Lincoln, 1856) 171.

13. A55 Ea. 1741.
14. J.W.F. Hill (ed.), *The Letters and Papers of the Banks Family of Revesby Abbey 1704-60* (LRS 45, Lincoln, 1952), 99.
15. Holderness, 'Rural Society', 90.
16. Hill, *Georgian Lincoln*, 149.
17. Holderness, 'Rural Society', 550.
18. Beastall, *Agricultural Revolution*, 133; C. Brears, *Lincolnshire in the 17th and 18th Centuries* (London, 1940), 122.
19. Lloyd, *Whichcot Letters*, 15; Beastall, *Agricultural Revolution*, 132.
20. Beastall, *Agricultural Revolution*, 21.
21. Holderness, 'Rural Society', 424.

Notes to Chapter 2

1. LAO, Monson, 7/91-9, Assize Calendars.
2. *Lincoln Date Book*, 176.
3. *LRSM*, 28 Apr. 1743.
4. *LRSM*, 19 May 1785.
5. *LRSM*, 6 Aug. 1745.
6. *Annual Register*, 1774, 145.
7. C. Bruyn Andrews (ed.), *The Torrington Diaries* (London, 1934) 2, 79.
8. *Annual Register*, 1760, 77.
9. *Lincoln Date Book*, 1777, 193.
10. *Annual Register*, 1775, 155.
11. Andrews, *Torrington Diaries*, 2, 345,358,362.
12. A165 M. 1769.
13. A141 M. 1763.
14. A169 Mc. 1744.
15. A69 Mc. 1744; A171 Ep. 1771; A173 M. 1771.
16. A191 Ep. 1776; Min. Ep. 1776.
17. A124 Ep. 1759; A133 M. 1761; A155 Ep. 1767; A171 Ep. 1771.
18. A141 M. 1763.
19. A73 Mc. 1745.
20. A77 M. 1745.
21. A192 Ea. 1776.
22. A181 M. 1773.
23. A64 M. 1743.
24. A161 M. 1768.
25. A85 Mc. 1748.
26. A166 M. 1768.
27. A80 M. 1747.
28. A110 M. 1755.

29. A186 Mc. 1774.
30. A194 Mc. 1776.
31. A158 M. 1767.
32. *Lincoln Date Book* (1753) 179.
33. Ibid., 1787, 211.
34. A61 Mc. 1747.
35. Adam Smith, *Lectures on Jurisprudence*, eds. R.L. Meek, D.D. Raphael, P.G. Stein (Oxford, 1978) 208.
36. A83 Ea. 1745.
37. A192 Ea. 1776.
38. A62 Ep. 1743; A152 Ea. 1766.
39. A153 M. 1766.
40. A180 Ea. 1773.
41. A53 Mc. 1740; A55 Ea. 1741.
42. A177 M. 1772; A203 Ep. 1779.
43. A176 Ea.1772.
44. A162 Mc. 1768; A84 M. 1748; A96 M. 1751.
45. A164 Ea. 1769; A179 Ep. 1773.
46. A187 Ep. 1775.
47. A199 Ep. 1778.
48. A92 M. 1750.
49. A199 Ep. 1778.
50. A200 Ea. 1778.
51. A183 Ep. 1774.
52. A174 Mc. 1771.
53. A193 M. 1776.
54. A106 Ea. 1754.
55. A187 Ep. 1775.
56. A112 Ep. 1756.
57. Hill, *Georgian Lincoln*, 116-7.
58. A192 Ea. 1776.
59. P.B. Munsche, *Gentlemen and Poachers. The English Game Laws 1671-1831*, (Cambridge, 1981) 7.
60. Sir W. Blackstone, *Commentaries on the Laws of England* (London, 1771) 4, 174.
61. Munsche, *Game Laws*, 7.
62. *LRSM*, 3 Jan. 1743; 24 Jan. 1743.
63. Munsche, *Game Laws*, 50.
64. Blackstone, *Commentaries*, 4, 174.
65. A164 Ea. 1769; A165 M. 1769.
66. Munsche, *Game Laws*, 85.
67. LAO Dixon 8/1/1-4, Justice Books of Thomas Dixon.
68. A159 Ep. 1768.

69. A139 Ep. 1763; A90 Ep. 1750.
70. A188 Ea. 1775.
71. LAO Massingberd-Mundy VII/2/88, miscellaneous correspondence.
72. Roger Longrigg, *The English Squire and his Sport* (London, 1977) 90.
73. *LRSM*, 25 Oct. 1770.
74. LAO, Crowle 5/2/2, Minutes of Crowle Manor Court, 20 Oct. 1774.
75. A88 M. 1749.
76. A71 Ea. 1745.
77. LAO, Massingberd Mundy, VII/2/88, 18 Nov. 1749.
78. Eleanor and Rex C. Russell, *Making New Landscapes in Lincolnshire* (Lincoln, 1983) 24, quoting Binbrook Enclosure Act, 1773.
79. A89 Mc. 1749.
80. A69 Mc. 1744; A63 Ea. 1743; A116 Ep. 1757; A91 Ea. 1750; A74 Ep. 1746.
81. LAO, Dixon 8/1/1, 10 Aug. 1789.
82. A85 Mc. 1748.
83. A161 M. 1768.
84. Anon, *An Enquiry into the Price of Wheat, Meat, etc.* (London, 1768), quoted in E. P. Thompson, 'The Moral Economy of the English Crowd', *Past and Present* 50 (Feb. 1971) 86.
85. *LRSM*, 10 Dec. 1767.
86. A82 Ep. 1748.
87. A64 M. 1743 and A70 Ep. 1745.
88. A82 Ep. 1748.
89. Min. Ea. 1775.
90. A150 Mc. 1765.
91. A53 Mc. 1740.
92. A59 Ea. 1742.
93. A124 Ep. 1759.
94. *LRSM*, 29 May 1766.
95. *LRSM*, 9 and 23 Oct. 1766.
96. A155 Ep. 1767.
97. Beckwith, *The Book of Gainsborough* (Buckingham, 1988) 96; A182 Mc. 1773; A206 Mc. 1779; A61 Mc. 1742: A143 Ep. 1764.
98. A95 Ea. 1751.
99. A74 Ep. 1745.
100. A181 M. 1773.
101. A54 Ep. 1741; A57 Mc. 1741.
102. A54 Ep. 1741.

103. A142 Mc. 1763; A87 Ea. 1749.
104. A139 Ep. 1763.
105. A77 Mc. 1746.
106. A153 M. 1766.
107. A131 Ep. 1761.
108. A62 Ep. 1743.
109. A152 Ea. 1766.
110. A61 Mc. 1742.
111. A189 M. 1775.
112. A139 Ep. 1763.
113. A200 M. 1778.
114. A93 Mc. 1750.
115. A110 M. 1775.
116. A166 Mc. 1769.
117. A94 Ep. 1751.
118. A57 Mc. 1741.
119. A93 Mc. 1750.
120. A188 Ea. 1775.
121. A64 M. 1743.
122. A76 M. 1746.
123. A185 M. 1774.
124. A192 Ea. 1776.
125. A93 Mc. 1750.
126. A165 M. 1769.
127. A200 Ea. 1778.

Notes to Chapter 3

1. LAO, Monson 7/92, Assize Calendars.
2. *Lincoln Date Book* (1785) 202.
3. *LRSM*, 4 Oct. 1770.
4. *Lincoln Date Book* (1722) 165.
5. Ibid., 1785, 204.
6. H. Best, *Personal and Literary Memorials* (London, 1829) 262.
7. Ibid., 262.
8. D. Hay, in D.Hay et al., *Albion's Fatal Tree* (London, 1975) 48.
9. *Annual Register* (1776) 183; (1778) 178.
10. Blackstone, *Commentaries*, 4, 475.
11. Lloyd, *Whichcot Letters*, 33.
12. James Obelkevich, *Religion and Rural Society: south Lindsey 1825-75* (Oxford, 1976) 320.
13. Hill, *Georgian Lincoln*, 60, n.2.
14. J.A. Penny, 'Mid-Lincolnshire Folklore', *LNQ* 2, (1890-1) 143.

15. P.R.G. Binnall , 'A Parish Clerk of Hibaldstow', *LNQ* 21-2, (1930-3) 69.
16. Blackstone, *Commentaries*, 4, 9.

Notes to Chapter 4

1. BL Add. Mss. 35601, f.227.
2. N. Landau, *The Justices of the Peace 1679-1760* (Berkeley, 1984).
3. BL Add. Mss. 35601, f.227.
4. Landau, *Justices*, 102.
5. J. Boswell, *The Life of Samuel Johnson* (London, 1906) 1, 267.
6. Landau, *Justices*, 104.
7. A186 Mc. 1774.
8. Lloyd, *Whichcot Letters*, 3.
9. Ibid., 17.
10. Sir L. Namier and J. Brooke (eds.), *The History of Parliament. The Commons 1754-90* (London, 1964) 3, 629.
11. Lloyd, *Whichcot Letters*, 31.
12. Namier and Brooke, *Parliament*, 3, 629.
13. Lloyd, *Whichcot Letters*, 35.
14. A148 Ea. 1765.
15. Namier and Brooke, *Parliament*, 3, 629.
16. E. Bentley Wood, 'Family of Stovin', *LNQ* 4, (1894-5) 90.
17. W.B. Stonehouse, *The History and Topography of the Isle of Axholme* (London, 1839)
18. Bentley Wood, 'Family of Stovin', 90.
19. Hill, *Georgian Lincoln*, 31-2.
20. Namier and Brooke, *Parliament*, 3, 501.
21. Beastall, *Agricultural Revolution*, 108.
22. Ibid., 108.
23. A54 Ep. 1741.
24. Namier and Brooke, *Parliament*, 3, 506.
25. Hill, *Banks Letters*, 184.
26. J.L. & B. Hammond, *The Village Labourer* (London, 1911) 14 .
27. LAO, Dixon 8/1/1-4.
28. A94 Ep. 1751.
29. LAO, Dixon 8/1/4.
30. Ibid.
31. Ibid.
32. Ibid.
33. Ibid.
34. A138 Mc. 1762.
35. A131 M. 1761.

36. Hill, *Georgian Lincoln*, 263.
37. A84 M. 1748.
38. A93 Mc. 1750.
39. A77 Mc. 1746.
40. A85 Mc. 1748.
41. A57 Ep. 1766.
42. A192 Ea. 1776.
43. This section is based on David Neave, 'Anti-Militia Riots in Lincolnshire, 1757 and 1796', *Lincolnshire History and Archaeology* 11 (1976) 21-6, and BL Add. Mss. 32874, ff. 158-62.
44. Neave, 'Anti-Militia Riots', 23.
45. Ibid., 26.

Notes to Chapter 5

1. Arthur Mee, *The King's England, Lincolnshire* (London, 1949) 352.
2. A202 Mc. 1778.
3. A60 Ea. 1742.
4. A71 Ea. 1745.
5. A187 Ep. 1775.
6. A178 Mc. 1772.
7. Min. Ep. 1763.
8. Min. Mc. 1747.
9. Min. M. 1776.
10. Min. M. 1747.
11. Peyton, *Minutes*, I, xliv.
12. Min. Ea. 1771.
13. Min. Ea. 1772.
14. Min. Ea. 1743.
15. A92 M. 1750.
16. Peyton, *Minutes*, I, xlviii.
17. E. Mansel Sympson, 'A Constable's Account for the Parish of Willoughton 1757', *LNQ* 5 (1896-8) 41.
18. A201 M. 1778.
19. A144 Ea. 1764.
20. A91 Ea. 1750
21. A108 Mc. 1754.
22. A112 Ep. 1756.
23. A187 Ep. 1775.
24. A54 Ep. 1741.
25. Min. Mc. 1742.
26. A146 Mc. 1764.

27. A187 Ep. 1775.
28. A148 Ea. 1765.
29. Peyton, *Minutes*, I, lxxiv.
30. Min Ea. 1747.
31. A113 Ea. 1756.
32. A116 Ep. 1757.
33. A55 Ea. 1741.
34. LAO, Minutes of Bradley Haverstoe Petty Sessions, 4 Feb. 1834; 18 Nov. 1834.
35. A94 Ep. 1751.
36. A77 Mc. 1746.
37. Peyton, *Minutes*, I, lxvii.
38. A57 Mc. 1741.
39. A203 Ep. 1779.
40. A168 Ea. 1770.
41. A144 Ea. 1764.
42. A62 Mc. 1768.
43. A76 M. 1746; A77 Mc. 1746.
44. A188 Ea. 1775.
45. A190 Mc. 1775.
46. A150 Mc. 1765.
47. A159 Ep. 1768.
48. A78 M. 1746.
49. A85 Mc. 1748.
50. A93 Mc. 1750; A204 Ea. 1779; Min. Ea. 1775.
51. Min. Ea. 1775 and Ea. 1776.
52. A112 Ep. 1756; A198 Mc. 1777.
53. A180 M. 1773.
54. A242 Mc. 1788; A176 Ea. 1772; A240 Ea. 1788; Min. M. 1775.
55. A242 Mc. 1788.
56. A192 Ea. 1776; A76 M. 1746.
57. A137 M. 1762; A139 Ep. 1763.
58. A239 Ep. 1788.
59. LAO, Monson 7/91-9.
60. Brears, *Lincolnshire*, 45.
61. Clive Holmes, *Seventeenth-Century Lincolnshire* (Lincoln, 1985) 22.

Notes to Chapter 6

1. Landau, *Justices*, 3
2. Obelkevich, *Religion and Rural Society*, 320.
3. Hill, *Georgian Lincoln*, 47.

4. W.A. Cragg, 'Roman Knights', *LNQ* 10 (1908-9), 177.
5. P. Gay, *The Enlightenment: an interpretation* (London, 1967) 69.
6. Hill, *Georgian Lincoln*, 94, n.3.
7. Ibid., 60.
8. Ibid., 60, n.2.
9. Andrews, *Torrington Diaries*, 2, n.3.
10. A. Young, *A Farmer's Tour through the East of England, 1771* (London 1773) 433-7; A. Young, *A General View of the Agriculture of Lincolnshire* (London, 1808) 56, 462.
11. Hill, *Georgian Lincoln*, 41.
12. A200 Ep. 1778.
13. A205 M. 1779.
14. A145 M. 1764.
15. Min. Mc. 1744.
16. A55 Ea. 1741.
17. Landau, *Justices*, 104.
18. Ibid., 8-9.
19. LAO, Kesteven Militia Papers, Military Lincolnshire, 1798.
20. LAO, Dixon 8/1/2.
21. Min. Ea. 1775.
22. A108 M. 1754.

Notes to Chapter 7

1. Min. M. 1777 and Ep.1778.
2. A135 Ep. 1762.

Notes to Chapter 8

1. Beastall, *Agricultural Revolution*; N.R. Wright, *Lincolnshire Towns and Industry 1700-1914* (Lincoln, 1982).
2. Wright, *Towns and Industry*, 39.
3. Brears, *Lincolnshire*, 155; Andrews, *Torrington Diaries*, 2, 378.
4. Andrews, *Torrington Diaries*, 2, 374 and 380.
5. Hill, *Lincoln*, 308-10.
6. J. Thirsk, *English Peasant Farming: the agrarian history of Lincolnshire from Tudor to Recent Times* (London, 1957) 252.
7. Young, *General View*, 7.
8. B.A. Holderness, 'The Agricultural Activities of the Massingberds of South Ormsby, 1638-1750', *Midland History*, I, no.3.
9. Hill, *Georgian Lincoln*, 129.
10. Wright, *Towns and Industry*, 60.
11. Holderness, 'Rural Society', 69ff.

12. Young, *General View*, 470.
13. J.C.D. Clark, *English Society 1688-1832* (Cambridge, 1985) 64-93.
14. Hammonds, *Village Labourer*, 69.
15. Holderness, 'Rural Society', 446.
16. Quincey, 'Tour', 208.
17. Ibid., 208.
18. Ibid., 207.
19. Anon., 'Extracts from the Diary of John Cragg of Threckingham - 1799', *LNQ* 11 (1910-11) 137.
20. Andrews, *Torrington Diaries*, 357, 359, 377, 409.
21. Young, *General View*, 7.
22. Ibid., 255.
23. Quincey, 'Tour', 206.
24. Ibid., 208.
25. Thirsk, *Farming*, 235.
26. A85 Mc. 1748.
27. A155 Ep. 1767.
28. A101 Mc. 1753.
29. A178 Mc. 1772.
30. A111 Mc. 1755; A172 Ea. 1771; A176 Ea. 1772.
31. A75 Ea. 1746.
32. A178 Mc. 1772.
33. A193 M. 1776.
34. A158 Mc. 1767.
35. A203 Ep. 1779.
36. A193 M. 1776.
37. A107 M. 1754.
38. A186 Mc. 1774.
39. *LRSM*, 14 July 1768.
40. G.S. Bagley, *Boston, Its Story and People* (Boston, 1986) 125.
41. A170 M. 1770.
42. A185 M. 1774; A187 Ep. 1775.
43. A178 Mc. 1772.
44. A189 M. 1775.
45. A187 Ep. 1775.

Notes to Chapter 9

1.   Min. Ea. 1771.
2.   Min. Mc. 1771.
3.   Min. Ea. 1772.
4.   Min. M. 1775.

5. Min. M. 1775.
6. Min. Mc. 1776.
7. Min. M. 1776.
8. Min. Ep. 1773
9. Min. Ea. 1773.
10. Min. Ea. 1775.
11. Min. Ep. 1776.
12. Min. Ep. 1776.
13. A195 Ep. 1777.
14. *LRSM*, 11 Aug. 1768; Hill, *Georgian Lincoln*, 71.
15. J. Howard, *The State of the Prisons in England and Wales* (Warrington, 1777) 296-7.
16. Min. Ea. 1773.
17. Min. Ea. 1773.
18. Min. Mc. 1773.
19. Min. Mc. 1774.
20. Min. Ea. 1771.
21. Beastall, *Agricultural Revolution*, 139; Hill, *Georgian Lincoln*, 119, 160.
22. Andrews, *Torrington Diaries*, 2, 321.